Succeed in OSCEs and Practical Exams

Succeed in OSCEs and Practical Exams: An Essential Guide for Nurses

Clair Merriman and Liz Westcott

 Open University Press

Open University Press
McGraw-Hill Education
McGraw-Hill House
Shoppenhangers Road
Maidenhead
Berkshire
England
SL6 2QL

email: enquiries@openup.co.uk
world wide web: www.openup.co.uk

and Two Penn Plaza, New York, NY 10121-2289, USA

First published 2010

A catalogue record of this book is available from the British Library

ISBN-13: 978-0-33-523734-0
ISBN-10: 0335237347

Library of Congress Cataloging-in-Publication Data
CIP data applied for

Typeset by RefineCatch Limited, Bungay, Suffolk
Printed in the UK by Bell & Bain Ltd, Glasgow

Fictitious names of companies, products, people, characters and/or data that
may be used herein (in case studies or in examples) are not intended to
represent any real individual, company, product or event.

Mixed Sources

Product group from well-managed
forests and other controlled sources
www.fsc.org Cert no. TT-COC-002769
© 1996 Forest Stewardship Council

FSC

The *McGraw·Hill* Companies

Praise for this book

"Clair Merriman and Liz Westcott have written this book so it feels like a companion to students who may be overwhelmed by the idea of having to take part in an OSCE, or being assessed through a simulated practice exercise. It is a mine of information that is not only applicable to nursing students, but to students from any discipline taking part in assessed practical sessions, even beyond healthcare from my experience in engineering education. The structure of the book makes it easy to read and very informative as it covers aspects such as learning theories, different OSCE formats and elements they may contain such as patient simulators and simulated patients, but it also includes some valuable tips to be well prepared for the day as well as some detailed example of stations. This book gives just the right emphasis on reflection about the OSCE experience once it is finished, and when one receives their feedback about their performance to correct their practice in the future. The framed key sentences throughout this book are very pertinent and perfectly complemented by a summary chapter. This book provides a fresh view on OSCEs and will be of great assistance to tutors about to embark on their use as an assessment strategy in nursing education, but more importantly, it is an essential guide for students."

Guillaume Alinier, NTF, SFHEA, School of Postgraduate Medicine,
University of Hertfordshire, Hatfield, UK

Contents

List of tables, diagrams and photographs

About the authors

Clair Merriman (MSc, BSc, Dip HE, RGN) is the Head of Professional Practice Skills, School of Health and Social Care, Oxford Brookes University. Clair has developed, implemented and evaluated the teaching, learning and assessment strategy for professional practice skills in the School. She ensures collaboration with students, service users and practice staff in terms of teaching and learning these skills. Clair manages 11 skills suites across two sites which support low- to medium-fidelity simulation. She has a national and international reputation for her work in simulated settings and OSCEs.

Liz Westcott (MSc, Dip Man, RNT, RGN) is Director of Pre-qualifying Learning and Development, School of Health and Social Care, Oxford Brookes University. Liz has led many developments in the School of Health and Social Care including the introduction of the nursing diplomas and foundation degrees. She is the executive lead for professional practice skills, practice education, recruitment and admissions, as well as interprofessional learning and collaborative practice.

Acknowledgements

The authors would like to thank the following: Angela Harper and Chris Bulman for their encouragement, support and critical reading; our families, in particular, Andrew, Alice and James, and Chris and Emma, for their support and understanding; the many lecturers at Oxford Brookes University who have developed the OSCEs, the checklists and marking criteria on which this book is based; and our learning technologists, Julia, Colleen, Toby, Irmgard and Kenny, for their support.

Introducing OSCEs and the book

1

Introduction

> The secret of getting ahead is getting started. The secret of getting started is breaking your complex overwhelming tasks into small manageable tasks, and then starting on the first one.
>
> Mark Twain (1835–1910)

> ### By the end of this chapter you will:
> ○ Be aware of what is on offer in this book.
> ○ Be aware of which order you will work through this book.
> ○ Feel a sense of purpose and control in your Objective Structured Clinical Examination (OSCE) preparation.

This book is for you if you are:

- needing help to prepare and succeed in your Objective Structured Clinical Examination (OSCE) or practical examination;
- a pre-registration nursing student;
- undertaking continuing professional development (CPD) as a registered nurse and have not taken an OCSE or practical examination before.

Up to now you may have been anxious and even alarmed about undertaking clinical skills teaching or simulated learning, and the prospect of an OSCE or practical examination may have petrified you. You can now be reassured, as this book is designed to ensure that you are well equipped to succeed in your OSCE or practical exam. The book does not presume that you know anything about OSCEs, and aims to be a practical guide to help you plan and succeed.

How to use this book

In this book we are talking directly to you. The book is aimed at helping you succeed in your OSCE and practical examination; however, it will only help if you fully engage with the content. Whether you are currently a student nurse or a registered nurse undertaking CPD, your studies will have challenged you and required you to make changes to your behaviour and attitude during your time at university. OSCEs may occur at various points in your course and they will challenge you personally and professionally. We aim throughout this book to help you to be an active participant in your learning so that you can feel a sense of autonomy and independence in the process.

OSCEs and practical examinations require you to be self-reliant, and this book can be a partner in your journey into:

- understanding your own learning style;
- understanding how reflection can give you greater insight into your practice;
- understanding how you can be empowered to improve your practice.

Each chapter starts with the outcomes you can expect to achieve through your reading, as well as what we hope is an inspiring quote. There are useful tips, key points, examples and case studies throughout the book, and each chapter concludes with a summary of the key points raised.

The book is aimed at preparing you for your OSCE or practical examination as part of a nursing course. These types of assessment are used to assess the *knowledge*, *skills* and *attitudes* that are required for safe and effective practice. Each chapter, where relevant, will make reference to the standards of proficiency for pre-registration nursing education (NMC 2004) and essential skills clusters (ESCs) (NMC 2007a, 2007b).

Essential skills clusters (ESCs)

The Nursing and Midwifery Council (NMC) requires certain outcomes to be achieved by the end of the first year, and certain proficiencies to be achieved at the end of pre-registration training in order for you to gain your professional nursing qualification. The ESCs were introduced by the NMC in September 2008 to ensure that students were proficient in the predetermined core requirements of care. The ESCs are UK-wide generic skills statements set out under the following broad headings:

- Care, compassion and communication
- Organizational aspects of care
- Infection prevention and control
- Nutrition and fluid balance control
- Medicines management

Each of these broad themes is fundamental for best practice, and is applicable to all four branches of nursing: adult, children's, learning disability and mental health.

Use of simulated learning in nursing courses

When nurse education moved into higher education (HE) in 1989, it shifted away from the apprenticeship model of training and a new type of course was introduced where continuous assessment of theory and practice was recommended. The dominant assessment model used historically to assess clinical competence was direct observation of clinical skills, however, more recently the NMC (2004, 2007c) has identified a greater need for joint responsibility for teaching and the assessment of clinical competence between the higher education institution (HEI) and clinical practice. The aim is to ensure that when you qualify or complete a CPD course you are fit for purpose and practice. As a result of this, there has been an increase in the use of 'skills laboratories', with the OSCE and/or practical examinations becoming widely employed to contribute to the assessment of clinical competence (NMC 2004, 2007c).

In addition, simulated learning has become more commonplace due to the reduction of practice placements and the increased pressures on the current workforce (Hall 2006). The teaching and assessment of clinical skills in a simulated learning environment have become an accepted part of pre- and post-registration nursing courses (Chatterjee 2004; Hilton and Pollard 2004; Wilson *et al.* 2005). At Oxford Brookes University we have used simulated learning to develop clinical skills since 1990 and this approach has been heightened by the introduction of ESCs by the NMC.

OSCEs and practical examinations are a form of assessment which allows you to demonstrate your skills, knowledge and attitude. Simulation allows you to practise your skills and demonstrate your knowledge and attitude in a safe and professional environment. This book will show you how you can reflect on these experiences and gain the most from the feedback you are given during them.

> OSCEs and practical examinations are a form of assessment which allows you to demonstrate your skills, knowledge and attitude.

Use of terminology

The term 'OSCE' from this point on will be deemed to include practical examinations. We are aware that the OSCE may be new to you, and so here we provide a simple definition and brief history of this examination.

Harden and Gleeson first introduced the OSCE into medical education in Scotland in 1975 (Carraccio and Englander 2000). Disciplines such as dentistry, chiropody, occupational therapy, physiotherapy, radiation therapy and more recently nursing also use OSCEs as a method of assessment.

The traditional OSCE consists of rotating students through a system of stations simulating a clinical reality (Ross *et al.* 1988; Nicol and Freeth 1998; Redfern *et al.* 2002). At each station, the student must perform a particular skill using a standardized patient, manikin, task trainer and/or a written scenario. Each station is constructed to assess a particular skill, such as history-taking, physical assessment, identifying a diagnosis, decision-making, client education or the performance of a technical procedure. The skills performed are assessed against a pre-established detailed checklist developed by a panel of clinical/education experts. The construction and application of the OSCE process vary in relation to the number of stations and the length of time allowed at each station, depending on the learning outcomes and objectives being assessed.

The term 'patient' will be used throughout this book, but can be replaced with 'client', 'person' or 'carer' as appropriate. The term 'manikin' will be used to denote mannequins, mannikins or dummies – are all terms used to describe life-sized training models.

Overview of chapters

Chapter 2, 'Understanding OSCEs: what you need to know', takes you through an OSCE and details the preparation you need to do before the exam. An OSCE is a method of simulating practice in a safe environment; therefore we will explore what a simulated learning environment is and the types of equipment that may be utilized. *Formative* and *summative* OSCEs are explored, including the differences between them and what is expected in both. Guidance is given on pre-reading, and how to find key texts that will inform your knowledge and skills related to the OSCE.

Chapter 3, 'Preparing for your OSCE: getting the most out of your learning', will help you to understand what you need to do in order to be successful in your OSCE. The *written information* from academic staff will be discussed so that you will understand what information you should expect to receive to inform you about the process of the OSCE, for example, possible timings of OSCEs, marking criteria and checklists. The chapter includes a section concerning the type of support available if you have a disability such as dyslexia or other specific learning difficulties, such as a sight or hearing impairment, or reduced mobility. The chapter will also help you to assess your own learning style, which will help you achieve better results in the long term.

Chapter 4, 'What to expect from your OSCE', concerns what your OSCE will require. There are many types of OSCE examination: 'simulated patient plus observed'; 'observed computer-assisted'; 'manikin plus observed'; 'manikin alone'; 'videoing'; 'computer only'; and 'oral/viva'. We will explore what you can expect from each type and the differences between them, as well as the varying approaches you will need to adopt to succeed in them. The chapter goes on to explain what you can expect from the following types of *simulated patient* and the differences between them, in addition to the varying approaches you will need to adopt:

- peers;
- actors;
- members of the public, both adults and children;
- practice staff;
- manikins;
- task trainers;
- computers.

You will read about the layout of a typical examination room and see photographic examples. The different types of examiner will be discussed, for example, academics, practitioners, patients and peers. Examiners' behaviours, roles and quality assurance options will also be discussed, for example, roaming moderators, cameras and external examiners. Finally, we look at how to maintain health and safety for yourself, simulated patients and examiners throughout the examination. For example, what to do if the fire alarm goes off or if unsafe practice is observed during your OSCE.

Chapter 5, 'Preparing for your OSCE: before and on the day', will help to ensure that you are fully prepared for your exam. It contains useful advice for calming your nerves and we will explain the physiology of stress to highlight that it is normal to feel this way prior to an OSCE, and demonstrate that stress can be successfully managed. We will look at when to arrive, time-keeping and management of travel arrangements as well as what to wear. We will also consider:

- freezing–unfreezing;
- relaxing;
- how to regroup if you go wrong;
- what to do if you feel unwell.

The chapter then examines the following strategies to improve your success rate:

- thinking carefully;
- improving your memory;
- considering the questions you may be asked before, during and after the OSCE;
- how to relate to the simulated patient or manikin.

Chapter 6, 'Sample OSCEs: adult basic life support, medicines management and aseptic non-touch technique', provides examples of OSCE stations that you may encounter during your course. The chapter demonstrates how you can break down each station, each checklist and the marking criteria and use this information to help prepare for, and therefore succeed in, your OSCE. An annotated checklist for each station is provided to show you what the examiner is looking for.

Chapter 7, 'After the OSCE has finished', talks about the post-OSCE process and discusses debriefing using feedback and reflection on your experience. The process of reflection is explained as are examples of various reflective models. The chapter discusses your relationship with other examined students, along with what to do if you are referred – or fail – and how to prepare for next time.

Chapter 8, 'Summary', provides a résumé of the chapter content, tips and key points. This will act as a quick reference guide when you need to revise your knowledge and understanding of OSCEs once you have read this book.

How to start

Now that you are aware of what is on offer in this book, you can decide in what order you will work through it. You may already have some experience of

OSCEs, simulated learning or university processes, or you may have no prior experience. In order to assist you in preparing for your OSCE in a timely manner we recommend that you complete the following self-assessment before continuing with this book. This will help you decide in which order you should study the chapters and how much time you should spend on each.

Self-assessment is a useful skill to master as it will enable you to develop the ability to examine and think critically about your practice. As with many new techniques, it is worth taking the time to practise, and the more times you evaluate your practice, the easier the process will become. Nicol and Macfarlane-Dick (2006) have also identified that well-organized self-assessment can result in real benefits in learning and achievement of goals.

> As with many new techniques, it is worth taking the time to practise, and the more times you evaluate your practice, the easier the process will become.

Once you have completed the self-assessment for each chapter, review your work and then try to prioritize the time you need to spend working through each chapter. The chapter with the shortest list is obviously a priority and will take you more time than the chapter with the longest list. You now need to set aside realistic times to work through each chapter. This will give you a sense of purpose and control and you will begin the process of becoming a self-reliant and autonomous practitioner and learner.

Use the self-assessment form presented in Table 1.1 as a basis for your self-assessment. We have put in the main content from each chapter and some examples, in italics, of how you might respond. Table 1.2 is a blank self-assessment form for you to fill in. You may like to revisit it once you have completed the book to see how much you have developed your practice.

When filling in the form, think about the type of statements that should be used in relation to knowledge and attitude:

- *Knowledge:* for this section use statements such as: 'I can discuss, describe, list, identify', etc.
- *Attitude:* for this part use statements such as: 'I can respond appropriately', 'act professionally', 'recognize the importance of', etc.

Table 1.1 Sample self-assessment form

Chapter 2	
Understanding OSCEs: what you need to know	
	Self-assessment • Simulated learning • Experiential learning • Advantages of OSCEs • Acquisition of skills • What is an OSCE and why use them? • Types of OSCE assessment
KNOWLEDGE I can discuss, describe, list, identify …	• *I can describe what is meant by simulated learning.* • *I have not heard of the term experiential learning before.* • *I am not sure why OSCEs are used as an assessment instead of an essay or exam.* • *I know an OSCE is an practical exam, however, I am not sure what the different types of OSCE are.*
ATTITUDE I can respond appropriately, *act* professionally, recognize the importance of …	• *Due to my lack of understanding of the above I am not sure how my attitude or behaviour influences this.* • *I do have a understanding of 'acting professionally' as we are bound by the NMC code of conduct.*

Chapter 3	
Preparing for your OSCE: getting the most out of your learning	
	Self-assessment
	• What is my learning style?
	• What types of OSCE do I know about?
	• What knowledge is expected of me in an OSCE?
	• What behaviour is expected of me in an OSCE?
KNOWLEDGE I can discuss, describe, list, identify ...	• *I have completed a learning style questionnaire before. I cannot remember what my learning style was called, however, I do remember I was someone who was motivated.*
	• *I currently cannot describe any OSCEs, although I am aware that I will have to complete OSCEs as part of my course.*
	• *I currently do not know what knowledge is expected of me.*
ATTITUDE I can respond appropriately, act professionally, recognize the importance of ...	• *I am aware that at university the ethos is that of adult learning, so I am aware that I need ensure that I understand what I am expected to achieve throughout my course.*
	• *I need to ascertain the behavioural and attitude traits I am required to demonstrate during the OSCEs.*

Chapter 4	
What to expect from your OSCE	
	Self-assessment
	• What layout of the room can I expect for my examination?
	• What types of simulated clients/models will be used during my assessment?
	• What types of examiners will I be assessed by?
	• What role-behaviour and performance are required of me in order to prepare me for this type of examination?
	• What mechanisms are used to ensure quality assurance?
KNOWLEDGE I can discuss, describe, list, identify …	• *I do not have any knowledge of the above as yet, however, I am hoping this book will help me with this!*
ATTITUDE I can respond appropriately, act professionally, recognize the importance of …	• *Once I am aware of what is expected of me I feel I will be able to respond appropriately, act professionally and of course understand the importance of this type of assessment.*

Chapter 5	
Preparing for your OSCE: before and on the day	
	Self-assessment
	• How should I prepare for my OSCE?
	• How can I perform to the best of my ability?
	• How will stress affect my performance?
	• How can I make the most use of the stress I am under to enhance my performance?
	• What are the 10 steps for preparation?
KNOWLEDGE I can discuss, describe, list, identify …	• *I have prepared for my A-level exams before, however, I am not sure how preparing for an OSCE differs, so I am hoping that working through this book will help me with this.*
	• *I think I know how I prepare for assessments, for example, I recently had an assessment on my level of fitness prior to being accepted onto the regional hockey team.*
	• *I am aware how I cope with stress, but I do not have specific strategies to do so.*
ATTITUDE I can respond appropriately, act professionally, recognize the importance of …	• *I think I can act appropriately and prepare and seek support when I need it, however, my past experience has not been at a university, so this may be different!*

Chapter 6	
Sample OSCEs: adult basic life support, medicines management and aseptic non-touch technique	
	Self-assessment
	• What types of OSCE will I come across in my training?
	• What type of marking criteria will I be assessed against?
	• What level of knowledge and skills do I need to display during the OSCE?
	• How many stations will I be examined at?
KNOWLEDGE I can discuss, describe, list, identify …	• *I do not know what type of OSCE I will come across; I just know that I will have them. I think my first OSCE will be on CPR.* • *I cannot answer any of the rest; I guess I need to do some investigating!*
ATTITUDE I can respond appropriately, act professionally, recognize the importance of …	• *I am aware that I lack of knowledge about this area and I need to do something about it!*

Chapter 7	
After the OSCE has finished	
	Self-assessment • What is good performance? • What is good feedback? • How can feedback empower me to improve my practice? • How can I reflect on my practice? • Which model should I use to help my reflection?
KNOWLEDGE I can discuss, describe, list, identify …	• *I do not know what a good performance is in relation to an OSCE.* • *I know good feedback should be constructive and direct me to how I can improve my work.*
ATTITUDE I can respond appropriately, act professionally, recognize the importance of …	• *I feel I have a good attitude to feedback as I always try and use the feedback I am given and act upon it.*

Table 1.2 Blank self-assessment form

Chapter 2	
Understanding OSCEs: what you need to know	
	Self-assessment • Simulated learning • Experiential learning • Advantages of OSCEs • Acquisition of skills • What is an OSCE and why use them? • Types of OSCE assessment
KNOWLEDGE I can discuss, describe, list, identify …	
ATTITUDE I can respond appropriately, act professionally, recognize the importance of …	

Chapter 3	
Preparing for your OSCE: getting the most out of your learning	
	Self-assessment • What is my learning style? • What types of OSCE do I know about? • What is knowledge expected of me in an OSCE? • What behaviour is expected of me in an OSCE?
KNOWLEDGE I can discuss, describe, list, identify …	
ATTITUDE I can respond appropriately, act professionally, recognize the importance of …	

Chapter 4	
What to expect from your OSCE	
	Self-assessment • What layout of the room can I expect for my examination? • What types of simulated clients/models will be used during my assessment? • What types of examiners will I be assessed by? • What role-behaviour and performance are required of me in order to prepare me for this type of examination? • What mechanisms are used to ensure quality assurance?
KNOWLEDGE I can discuss, describe, list, identify …	
ATTITUDE I can respond appropriately, act professionally, recognize the importance of …	

Chapter 5	
Preparing for your OSCE: before and on the day	
	Self-assessment
	• How should I prepare for my OSCE?
	• How can I perform to the best of my ability?
	• How will stress affect my performance?
	• How can I make the most use of the stress I am under to enhance my performance?
	• What are the 10 steps for preparation?
KNOWLEDGE I can discuss, describe, list, identify …	
ATTITUDE I can respond appropriately, act professionally, recognize the importance of …	

Chapter 6	
Sample OSCEs: adult basic life support, medicines management and aseptic non-touch technique	
	Self-assessment
	• What types of OSCE will I come across in my training?
	• What type of marking criteria will I be assessed against?
	• What level of knowledge and skills do I need to display during the OSCE?
	• How many stations will I be examined at?
KNOWLEDGE I can discuss, describe, list, identify …	
ATTITUDE I can respond appropriately, act professionally, recognize the importance of …	

Chapter 7	
After the OSCE has finished	
	Self-assessment • What is good performance? • What is good feedback? • How can feedback empower me to improve my practice? • How can I reflect on my practice? • Which model should I use to help my reflection?
KNOWLEDGE I can discuss, describe, list, identify …	
ATTITUDE I can respond appropriately, act professionally, recognize the importance of …	

Good luck in your OSCE! We hope that you will find this book useful

Chapter summary

1 OSCE means Objective Structured Clinical Examination.

2 This book will help you to:
   • understand your own learning style;
   • understand how reflection can provide greater understanding of your practice;
   • understand how you can be empowered to improve your practice.

3 The book is divided into eight chapters.

4 There are a variety of top tips throughout the book.

5 Each chapter has a chapter summary.

6 The teaching and assessment of clinical skills in a simulated learning environment have increased.

7 There is a wide variety of simulated patient types.

8 There is a wide variety of simulated settings.

9 Try to undertake a self-assessment of your current knowledge and skills.

10 Self-assessment is a useful tool to master as it will enable you to develop the ability to examine and think critically about your practice.

Understanding OSCEs: what you need to know

2

There are no secrets to success. It is the result of preparation, hard work, and learning from failure.

Colin Powell (1937–)

By the end of this chapter you will:

○ Be prepared for learning in the simulated learning environment.
○ Be clear about the purpose of an OSCE assessment as part of your nursing course.
○ Have read a range of practical tips and advice on what you need to do in order to be successful in your OSCE.

The simulated learning environment

Simulated learning environments utilized by your university, such as clinical skills laboratories, simulated wards, home environments and communication suites, will provide you with the opportunity to develop your psychomotor, clinical and decision-making skills. The nursing profession makes extensive use of the three major learning domains/skills – cognitive, psychomotor and affective – which we will now explain.

- *Cognitive (knowing) domain:* this focuses on knowledge acquisition and intellectual skills and abilities (e.g. interpreting and acting upon a patient's vital signs).
- *Psychomotor (doing) domain:* this is related to clinical skills that require varying levels of well-coordinated physical activity and precise manipulative procedures (e.g. taking a patient's blood pressure).
- *Affective (feeling) domain:* this deals with feelings, emotions, mindsets and values, including attitudes for personal and professional development

(e.g. displaying appropriate behaviour when caring for a patient, such as gaining informed consent prior to taking a patient's blood pressure).

In order for you to deliver effective patient care you will need to intertwine all three of these skills. However, they will be facilitated, taught or assessed via an OSCE, separately or together, depending on the learning outcomes of the session and the stage of your course. Within the nursing documentation these domains or skills are often referred to as 'knowledge', 'skill' and 'attitude', and from now on that is how we will refer to them.

Spending facilitated learning time in the simulated learning environment will enable you to apply practice knowledge and develop critical thinking as well as increase your confidence. Simulated learning gives you the opportunity to practise skills and develop your knowledge of and attitude to real-life health and social care situations in a safe, friendly and structured environment. In the case of nursing, this environment can be a skills laboratory, communication suite, a suite of rooms, a classroom or via virtual computer-generated programs. The sophistication of these rooms can vary from basic to high-fidelity, depending on the learning objectives being addressed and the facilities your university has access to.

> Simulation allows you to practise clinical and communication skills in a safe environment.

The simulated learning environment will give you the opportunity to learn clinical skills such as how to take a manual blood pressure and/or work through scenarios that are based on real-life situations and that resemble authentic experiences in the practice setting, such as caring for a patient whose health is deteriorating. The scenarios in a real-life or a virtual setting may respond to your actions so that a patient's condition/behaviour can improve or worsen following your interventions. For example, if a patient is hypoxic and you fail to apply oxygen therapy, they may become unconscious or have a respiratory arrest.

This facility has the great advantage of being able to bring uncertainty and unpredictability into your scenarios. This allows you to work through such situations in a safe environment before practising them in your clinical practice placement. In some instances the simulated learning environment will enable you to learn skills related to training in complex or challenging procedures – for example, restraining and sedating a patient who has been sectioned under the Mental Health Act.

> Simulation allows you to learn skills related to complex and/or challenging situations in a controlled setting.

Communication skills

Communication skills may be developed using a suite of rooms with two-way mirrors or video systems. This allows other students, as well as your tutors, to observe you and provide feedback. In many settings your interventions can be video-recorded and viewed later by you and your tutors. This aids your reflection and reinforces your learning of the experience. You have the opportunity to review decisions and alter them, because you can repeat the scenario, pause, slow down or speed up. You will have almost instant feedback from your tutors and peers and a chance to reflect on your practice in the OSCE.

> The simulated learning environment allows video-recording to aid feedback and reflection.

What is simulation?

'Simulation' means resembling reality. In nursing, simulated practice learning aims to replicate an aspect of, or all of the components of, a clinical situation so that you will be better able to understand and manage the situation if/when it occurs in clinical practice. An OSCE is a form of simulated practice that takes place in the university or formal academic setting. Therefore it is essential that, as part of your preparation, you take part in any practice simulated sessions that your university offers. By undertaking learning in these environments prior to your OSCE, you will become familiar with:

- the environment;
- any equipment you will be required to use;
- being observed by academic staff or peers.

For learning to be effective in the skills laboratory setting, it must be carefully integrated with the theoretical and practical aspects of the course, otherwise this learning will be less meaningful and not appear relevant. Within this environment you will be exposed to a range of equipment. This will include 'task trainers', which are parts of a manikin designed for you to learn a particular clinical skill – for example, a specific torso to learn the skill of urinary catheterization. It may also include very sophisticated high-fidelity manikins that can be programmed to respond to affective clinical changes – for example, 'MetiMan'.

However, for non-invasive procedures or physical examination, interviewing or patient education, 'standardized patients' – individuals who are trained to act as a patient – can be used. You will learn more about how and when they will be used in your OSCE in Chapter 3.

> Simulation must integrate theory and practice to be effective.

Simulation practical consent form

A very valuable part of learning in the simulated learning environment is putting yourself in the role of the patient. This will help you to begin to make sense of and understand what it may feel like to be a patient. In this case you act as the patient for your peers. Prior to your course starting you may be asked to sign a 'simulation practical consent form', as you may be examined and be subject to non-invasive investigations such as recording blood pressure. This form is an important part of the health and safety component of the course as it alerts you to the need to undertake simulation and what this may entail. It also emphasizes the fact that you may find an abnormality in yourself or others when engaging in simulation and you need to know how to report this. An example of such a form is shown below.

Consent form for simulation of practice, including role play and practical procedures

As is the normal practice in health and social care education, students will take part in practical procedures as part of their training during the academic components of their courses. Students will take part in these activities both as practitioner and as patient/service user. It is therefore a condition of any offer that the university makes of a place on one of its health and social care courses that you agree to take part in these activities and to the following terms and conditions in relation to your participation by signing this form. For the avoidance of doubt, any reference in this form to a practical procedure/s is the simulation of practice, including role play.

1   I understand that, whilst an experienced lecturer will introduce each practical session and the known risks and limitations of the practical procedures will be explained to me, it is my responsibility to be aware of any precautions and contraindications for each of the practical procedures.

2   Depending on the procedure, it may be necessary for me to remove clothing which may otherwise prevent observation and/or examination. Appropriate clothing and footwear should be worn for all practical sessions (i.e. loose clothing and flat, enclosed shoes). For the avoidance of doubt, it will not be necessary for me to remove clothing if I am studying the following pre-registration courses: nursing and midwifery, occupational therapy, operating department practitioner, social work, or if I am studying the following post-registration/graduate courses: non-medical prescribing, minor illness and injury management.

3   Every effort will be made to respect my dignity, moral, religious and cultural beliefs.

4   A video-recording system has been installed in the communication suite and some of the skills laboratories in the School of Health and Social Care. The aim of this is to provide students and lecturers with the opportunity to record students' activities for the purpose of feedback and assessment. The system is called SMOTS – Scotia Medical Observation and Training System.

The recording equipment operates on a continuous cycle. The video stream can be watched live or retrospectively at the viewing station in the labs. The centrally stored video stream is automatically destroyed after approximately seven days. Access to the recordings is restricted to named academic staff and skills laboratory technicians. Students do not have independent access to video streams and will only be shown these for learning purposes at their own request.

It is anticipated that practical procedures, case presentations, OSCEs and practical exams will be recorded. These will be downloaded and stored securely by the module leader on a password-protected file and in a locked cupboard. This footage may be accessed by the external examiner of the module for purposes of auditing students' work and parity of lecturers' marking. These recordings will be destroyed when results have been ratified by the examination board. Video footage will be automatically destroyed after seven days unless a student specifically requests that it is downloaded. In this case the module leader will keep the recording on a password-protected file and in a locked cupboard until the student and base group leader concerned have finished with it, after which time it will be destroyed.

Given the sensitive nature of recording students acting as models/patients/ service users it is anticipated that students and lecturers will accord with the same standards as is expected by professional and regulatory bodies and practitioners towards patients and colleagues in practice, including the measures taken to store securely the data described above.

I understand that if I am participating in a practical procedure in any of the skills laboratories with SMOTS, recording may take place.

5   In circumstances where I feel unable to take part in any of the practical procedures for whatever reason, I must inform the member of staff who is facilitating the session at the earliest opportunity.

6   I understand that, prior to any practical procedure, I must inform the member of staff who is facilitating the session of any health condition that may affect my participation.

7   I understand that I must inform the member of staff who is facilitating the session should I experience any symptoms of being unwell or injury during a practical procedure and that he or she must stop the procedure immediately should I indicate such symptoms or request that it should be stopped.

8   I understand that I have the right to withdraw from a practical procedure at any time and that, if I am studying the following pre-registration courses: nursing and midwifery, occupational therapy, operating department practitioner, social work, or if I am studying the following post-registration/graduate courses: non-medical prescribing or minor illness and injury management, I exercise my right to withdraw in respect of my role as patient/service user, and the exercise of that right shall be without prejudice.

9   In the event of something being discovered with regard to my health during a practical procedure, I understand that I must inform the member of staff who is facilitating the session and that it is my responsibility to seek further specialist advice from appropriate medical sources. I also understand that in the event of such information being discovered, whether as a result of a practical procedure or my responsibilities under any paragraph of this form, or otherwise, which might affect my ability to act as a patient/service user or undertake clinical practices safely, the member of staff facilitating the session may, after discussion with me, make a referral to occupational health and I must inform my personal tutor of the outcome of such a referral.

10 I understand that, in the event of the development of any recognized complication either during or subsequent to a practical procedure, the procedure will be stopped and/or not repeated on that occasion. With the mutual agreement of myself and the member of staff who is facilitating the session the procedure may be undertaken at a later date. The university will give formal advice regarding the management of any complication in the first instance. In the event of any complication arising, the member of staff facilitating the session undertakes to inform the relevant university personnel and make an appropriate entry in the incident book of the university's School of Health and Social Care.

11 I understand that I must inform the university of any change in my health status occurring during the course subsequent to my initial occupational health screening.

12 While the university will make reasonable adjustments to accommodate me, I understand that, subject to Paragraph 8 above, if a discovery is made as indicated in Paragraph 9 of this form or I withdraw from a practical procedure, I may not be permitted to complete my course.

13 I acknowledge that the university will not be liable in circumstances where I have failed to abide by these terms and conditions.

Declaration

I have read and fully understand the above. I agree to take part in the practical procedures and to the terms and conditions in relation to my participation as a practitioner or patient/service user.

Signature:

Full name:

Date:

Experiential learning

The ethos of the simulated learning environment is based upon *experiential learning* (Studdy *et al.* 1994; Quinn 2000; Fry *et al.* 2001). Experiential learning occurs in two forms in nursing education:

- in the form of structured and pre-planned practical work incorporating reflection on your experience in the laboratory;
- when you reflect on real experiences from the clinical environment and re-enact these in this environment.

The OSCE examination takes place in the simulated learning environment and is a structured practical experience that is used as an opportunity for you to demonstrate your knowledge, skills and attitude to the examiner. Although OSCEs are exams, they are still an invaluable learning opportunity for you, because you can use the feedback given by the examiner in order to improve your knowledge, skills and attitudes. The feedback that you should receive during any simulated learning, including your OSCE, and the reflection this should prompt, is said to be the most valuable part of the experience. Chapter 7 discusses in greater detail how to utilize both feedback and reflection to help you succeed in your OSCE.

> Although OSCEs are exams, they are also essential experiences for learning and reflection.

How does simulation fit into student learning?

You may well have heard of simulators used in the training of, for example, surgeons and aircraft pilots, and a similar principle has been adopted in the training of nursing students. However, simulation is not a recent invention, as throughout history representations in clay and stone have been used to demonstrate clinical features of disease states and their effects on humans. Examples have been found from many cultures and continents; indeed, the first medical simulators were simple models of human patients.

Simulation has developed into sophisticated computer-generated programs to enable, for example, surgeons to practise and perfect techniques before trying them on real patients, or pilots to experience complex situations before meeting them in a real-life crisis scenario.

Simulation of practice also came to the forefront due to changes in the health needs of hospitalized patients as a result of different illness patterns (Bujack *et al.* 1991), which led to shorter stays as inpatients in hospitals. Along with this there was an increase in clinical sophistication and an increase of critically ill patients in hospitals, paralleled by a shift in patient care to the community. This resulted in nursing students having less access to patients. At the same time, it was found that increasing numbers of nursing students were spending more time in academic settings.

By the mid-1990s this resulted in students having fewer opportunities to gain essential skills to enable them to progress to being independent, competent practitioners (Studdy *et al.* 1994). Added to this, the White Paper, *Making a Difference* clearly stated that the National Health Service (NHS) needed practitioners who were fit for purpose, with excellent skills, and the knowledge and ability to provide the best care possible (DoH 1999).

To try and respond to these changes the new century saw universities set up skills laboratories or skills centres to help bridge the gaps identified. Since then, evaluation of this method of teaching, learning and assessment has confirmed that clinical skills laboratories and simulation of practice have become an important component of nurse training (Bradshaw and Merriman 2008).

> Simulated learning has been with us for hundreds of years. It is used more than ever in this century to enable students to gain the most from their practice experience.

NMC role in simulated learning

The use of simulated learning and assessment has more recently been given greater credibility by the NMC (2007a, 2007b, 2007c), with the publication of the ESCs and the following statement: 'Nursing students will have more varied opportunities to develop direct care skills, following the Nursing and Midwifery Council's (NMC) decision to promote simulated practice learning for better preparing students for practice.'

This declaration followed a project involving more than 6,000 students from 13 pilot sites in UK universities. It tested out principles for the safe and effective use of simulated practice learning, using some of the time normally spent learning in the clinical area. Consequently, simulated learning opportunities may now be incorporated into pre-registration undergraduate nursing programmes. A maximum of 300 hours of the compulsory 2,300 direct practice hours may be taken up by simulated learning. As the NMC states, this environment cannot replace clinical practice experience but, if used correctly, can complement it.

In the pre-registration nursing curriculum the NMC allow for up to 300 hours of the 2,300 hours of direct patient care to be experienced in simulated learning.

Advantages of OSCEs

The following are some of the advantages of OSCEs and why the OSCE has been chosen as an assessment strategy as opposed to other forms of assessment.

- OSCEs convey a strong message to you about why clinical skills are important.
- OSCEs have been extensively researched and found to have academic rigour for both formative and summative assessment in health professional education because they are conducted using robust processes (number of stations, preparation of simulated patients/examiners, global judgement alongside checklist).
- OSCEs provide you, your clinical placement and the university with useful information about your knowledge, skills and attitude in relation to identified clinical skills.
- The assessment of predetermined essential skills is a requirement for you to demonstrate that you have met the NMC ESCs.
- OSCEs encourage a collaborative approach between HEIs and practice in the creation of nurses who are 'fit for purpose'.
- OSCEs are adaptable across professions, clinical skills and academic levels.
- OSCEs have potential for self-, peer and academic feedback.
- OSCEs promote development of functioning knowledge.

OSCEs allow you to demonstrate knowledge, skills and attitude related to a particular clinical skill in a safe environment.

Acquisition of skills

When you are working in a simulated learning environment and preparing for your OSCE, you will be acquiring new skills and refining skills you have already learned in practice. Having ownership of the acquisition of new skills and the related knowledge that goes alongside this is key to you succeeding in your OSCE.

One model you may find useful to help make sense of your acquisition of skills is the *conscious competence model*. This model's origins are not certain, however, some sources have indicated that its formal structure and development stem from the Gordon Training International organization in the USA (1970). This approach is also referred to by Howell and Fleishman (1982) and you will find it has some similarities with Bloom's taxonomy of learning (1956) in terms of the acquiring of cognitive, affective and psychomotor skills. Further development of the model (Baume 2004) has resulted in the five-stage process we will introduce you to here.

Stage 1: Unconscious incompetence

When you first start learning your clinical practice skills you will be at Stage 1, deemed *unconscious incompetence*: you are not aware of the skills you need to learn. It is clearly essential when you begin the process of skill acquisition that you understand the need for skills to be learned and it is as a result of this that you will become receptive to new learning. For example, you may not realize why numeracy is important for nurses because you are unable to put it into context. It is not until you use your numeracy skills that you understand the importance of them – for example, when calculating medication requirements, when assessing a patient's body mass index (BMI), when completing a fluid balance chart or when taking and recording vital signs.

> Stage 1: unconscious incompetence – you are not aware of the skills you need to learn.

In practice or the simulated learning environment your mentors and tutors recognize this stage and therefore do not assume prior knowledge. However, it is essential that you develop awareness of which skills you are not confident with, whether prior to learning a new skill or once you think you have learned one but are not competent in it.

You could also interpret Stage 1 behaviour as a mind-set you may adopt after your OCSE if you reach the stage of thinking you do not need to improve at all. This could still be thought of as unconscious incompetence, in that you may not have insight into the fact that you are not competent. Often students will have that 'lightbulb moment' when they finally understand all the components of a skill and the need to learn it, and this can occur at any stage of this model.

Benner's stages of clinical competence

The learning stages model has many similarities with Benner's stages of clinical competence in her 'Novice to Expert' model (1984). Benner based her model on the work of Dreyfus and Dreyfus (1986). They drew on their different outlooks as a computer scientist and a philosopher and developed a useful five-stage model. Benner's work has been instrumental to nurses understanding how to develop their levels of competence and therefore you will find it useful to look at the two models in parallel.

The stage of unconscious incompetence is similar to Benner's 'beginners' stage. A beginner does not have any experience of the situations or skills that they are expected to undertake. Novices learn rules to help them undertake a new skill and these rules do not have a context and are not related to anything the student has undertaken before. Therefore the rules tend to be applied across the board. This rule-governed approach to practice is therefore often very inflexible and limited. In relation to an OSCE this stage would be represented by you not knowing what an OSCE is or what skills are required to undertake it.

> Stage 1 (Benner): no experience of the situations or skills you are expected to undertake.

Stage 2: conscious incompetence

Stage 2 is deemed 'conscious incompetence' and is where you begin to understand the need to develop a skill and recognize your own lack of knowledge and skills. You also realize that by developing this skill, your practice will improve. For example, you have an OSCE testing your ability to carry out a manual blood pressure measurement. Although you are able to carry out the clinical skill of taking a blood pressure and inform the examiner of the correct reading, when you are questioned on the physiology of blood pressure you are unable to give a concise and correct answer and therefore fail the OSCE. Following feedback you recognize the need to increase your knowledge of the anatomy of the heart and the physiology of blood pressure. Conscious incompetence is an important watershed in understanding your ability and recognizing how much you need to learn. It can be a little scary when you realize that you may have been undertaking skills incorrectly for a while without knowing it, as in Stage 1. However, you have now recognized that you need to learn how to be competent and you are now able to start on the journey to competence in whichever skill you are learning.

> Stage 2: conscious incompetence – you understand the need to develop a skill and recognize your lack of knowledge.

This stage is also akin to Benner's 'advanced beginner stage'. This is when you can demonstrate just about acceptable performance of a skill. You are starting to base your practice on previous experience and learned skills rather than just the 'rules'. You are also starting to use a set of principles to guide your performance.

Stage 3: conscious competence

Stage 3 may well be the stage you reach for the OSCE and is deemed 'conscious competence'. You are able to undertake the skill and have knowledge of the need for the skill. In the above example, at this stage you are able provide a concise and correct answer concerning the physiology of blood pressure and therefore pass the OSCE. However, this knowledge is not yet 'second nature' to you and so you may not have reached the fourth stage, that of 'unconscious competence'. Now is the time to really refine your skills and knowledge. Take your time when performing a particular skill, learn it well and thoroughly, and in time it will become second nature.

> Stage 3: conscious competence – you can undertake a skill and have some knowledge base behind it.

This stage is a little like learning to drive when you are able to change gear but are thinking about when to do this all the time rather than just driving on instinct and experience. It is akin to Benner's 'competence' stage and can be illustrated by a student who has been undertaking a skill for quite a period of time and has a conscious understanding of how they are performing that skill. As a result the student will tend to consciously analyse their actions and enhance their efficiency and organizational ability. The competent student may not yet have enough experience to be able to translate all their skill to another similar situation but is well on the way to doing this.

Stage 4: unconscious competence

At Stage 4 you will be able to undertake a skill without having to think through exactly what you are doing all the time. At this stage you will be more able to interact with your patient as you will not be thinking about every step you need to take when performing a particular procedure. You will also be more adept at picking up on non-verbal clues from your patient as you will have the ability to concentrate more fully on their needs. You would pass the OSCE and the examiners' feedback would be very complimentary.

> Stage 4: unconscious competence – you can undertake the skill without thinking about what you are doing all the time.

This stage is akin to Benner's 'novice to expert': you are proficient and understand skills as complete entities rather than in terms of sections and tasks. When you are proficient you can comprehend a situation in its totality because you recognize its meaning in respect of long-term goals. The proficient practitioner has learned from experience how to modify their behaviour and skills in relation to differing situations. At this stage you will be able to modify your practice to allow for the unexpected. This is particularly useful in OCSEs when they are based on a clinically changing situation.

Stage 5: reflective competence

Reflective competence encourages the practitioner to delve more deeply into their abilities and review the literature and theory in terms of the skill concerned. Stage 5 is an opportunity for deeper analysis of your knowledge, skills and attitudes. As a result you will move to a higher level of performance than that expected of you in a pre-registration OSCE but highly desirable for post-registration studies or postgraduate courses such as non-medical prescribing or minor illness and injury management. Whatever level you are being assessed at, it's good to always aim to perform *above* the level required.

> Stage 5: reflective competence – able to use reflection to delve more deeply into your competence.

This stage is paralleled by Benner's 'expert performer'. Here you are able to grasp intuitively most skills situations. You will have a deeper understanding of what is required, and this understanding has been gained from repeated experience and reflection. You may also act more intuitively in your practice. You will still be guided by protocols but your understanding is such that you are now able to question practice and ask *why* skills are being undertaken in a particular way. At this level you will also be able to use analytical skills to think about situations you have not come across before.

Table 2.1 illustrates the conscious competence model stages and Benner's stages of clinical competence.

Table 2.1 The conscious competence model and Benner's stages of clinical competence

	Incompetence	*Competence*
Unconscious	Stage 1 You are not aware of the need to learn a skill *or* you think you have learned the skill and have no insight that you are not yet competent	Stage 4 You are able to undertake the skill without thinking about it all the time You are able to multi-task while undertaking the skill This is the stage ideally you will want to be at on completion of your course or when undertaking an advanced OSCE
	Benner: novice	***Benner: proficient***
Conscious	Stage 2 You are aware of the need to learn a skill but do not have the knowledge base You know that your practice will improve if you learn the skill	Stage 3 You are able to be proficient in the skill but need to think about each stage You will need to have at least reached this stage to succeed in your OSCE
	Benner: advanced beginner	***Benner: competent***
Reflection		Stage 5 You are able to reflect on your competence level and identify how you can improve your knowledge base and attitude by using literature and analysis
		Benner: expert

What is an OSCE?

Now that you have thought about how you acquire your skills and knowledge, we are going to explain the role of the OSCE in the assessment of that knowledge and those skills.

The OSCE was originally developed in Dundee in the mid-1970s by Harden and Gleeson (1979), to assess clinical competence of trainee doctors by rotating them through a range of 'stations' where they were assessed on a simulated clinical situation using precise sets of criteria. Shortly after Harden first described and introduced the OSCE into medical education in Britain, Europe and North America, extensive research began to demonstrate the excellent statistical properties of this approach (Regehr *et al.* 1998; Reznick *et al.* 1998). As a result, in the late twentieth century, OSCEs were said to represent the 'gold standard' for medical student assessment (Hodges 2003).

It is from this underlying assumption – that medical clinical competence could finally be tested in a precise and reproducible way – that Ross *et al.* (1988) concluded that the OSCE could be a valuable tool in assessing clinical skills in nursing. Since then it has been subject to extensive research with many papers applauding it as a reliable and valid assessment of clinical skills for nursing students (Hulett and Gilder 1986; Ross *et al.* 1988; O'Neill and McCall 1996; Nicol and Freeth 1998; Marshall and Harris 2000; Mossey *et al.* 2001; Alinier 2003).

The OSCE is thought to be a rigorous way of identifying your strengths and limitations in clinical competence. Within the literature, debate continues as to whether this model of assessment is superior to more traditional models, such as continual clinical assessment, multiple choice papers or the essay (Nicol and Freeth 1998; Shanley 2001).

A document published by the Commonwealth of Australia (National Review of Nurse Education Australia 2002) argued that the use of OSCEs within pre-registration nursing programmes produced students who were more 'competent' to learn in and from practice. It was also felt that this approach had significantly contributed to both the risk management of the service and public protection. The application of the OSCE to nursing has been positively evaluated in numerous studies (Knight 1998; Knight and Mowforth 1998; Khattab and Rawlings 2001; Walters and Adams 2002; NMC 2007a, 2007b, 2007c).

The student's perspective

Several studies have explored the student's perspective to ascertain whether OSCEs motivate students to learn clinical skills (Ross *et al.* 1988; Bujack *et al.* 1991; Bramble 1994; Govaerts *et al.* 2001; Alinier 2003; Furlong *et al.* 2005; Major

2005). They all concluded that the majority of students agreed that the OSCE exam-ination motivated them to learn the clinical skills being examined. The OSCE is also found to send a strong message to students that the acquisition of practical skills is important to becoming a competent professional nurse (Ramsden 2002).

However, it could also be argued that this is a weakness of the OSCE exami-nation as students may choose to focus on these clinical skills and ignore others. This is acknowledged by While (1994), Redfern *et al.* (2002) and Brookes (2004) who suggest that professional practice is multi-dimensional and com-bining multiple methods of assessment adds breadth and depth.

Students also commented that they felt safe with this approach because all expectations of them are clear and up-front. They know exactly what they are being tested on from the first day of the course and have opportunities to prac-tise the skills and learn the concepts deemed to be critical.

Advocates of the OSCE as an assessment strategy have argued for its implementation into the pre-registration curriculum. As a result the OSCE examination is increasingly being incorporated into pre-registration pro-grammes (Nicol and Freeth 1998; Redfern *et al.* 2002; NMC 2004, 2007a, 2007b, 2007c; Major 2005).

> Students feel safe with OSCEs because all expectations of them are clear and up-front.

Why use an OSCE?

OSCEs are just one of the types of assessment that may be used to assess you. You are assessed for a number of different reasons:

- to motivate you;
- to create learning opportunities;
- to provide feedback (for you and your tutors);
- to provide you with a grade;
- to act as a quality assurance mechanism (both for internal and external systems).

An OSCE will have been chosen as the assessment strategy for a number of reasons, usually because when it comes to practical outcomes the only sensible way of really assessing whether an outcome has been learned is through watch-ing you actually perform it. Other reasons why this approach is used include ensuring that you are adequately prepared with the relevant skills, knowledge and attitude before undertaking a skill in your area of practice. The OSCE also eases the burden of assessment from the practice area, measures your fitness for practice and assesses a skill that is essential for you to be competent in patient safety.

Types of assessment

Assessment will play a crucial role during your time at university. It is important because:

- it will determine much of the work you undertake;
- it will focus your approach to learning;
- it is an indication of which aspects of the course are valued most highly.

There is a difference between OSCE practice assessments, which are mainly intended to help you learn, and are called *formative*, and an OSCE final examination which is intended to identify how much has been learned by you and is called *summative*.

Formative OSCE assessments

Formative OSCEs are usually undertaken part of the way through your course or module. Such an assessment will involve your receiving feedback on your current skills, knowledge and attitude, which you can use to improve your future performance. The formative OSCE, if it precedes a summative OSCE, will also give you invaluable guidance and the time, if needed, to improve on any weak areas identified by you and the tutor.

You will gain valuable feedback about your performance and what and how you can improve in order to gain as good a mark as possible in your summative OSCE. You should use the time between the formative attempt and the summative attempt to build on your strengths and learn from your limitations through the feedback you are given. Ideally your formative attempt(s) should be staged throughout your course or module, so that you have enough time to act on the feedback that is provided by the examiners.

> Formative OSCEs give you constructive feedback and allow you to make improvements before the final summative attempt.

The formative OSCE is therefore an assessment that is used to help you and your tutors gauge the strengths and limitations of your performance, while there is still time to take action for improvement. Typically you will receive feedback expressed in words and/or in written form and you are not normally given a mark or grade.

Many people say that formative assessment is more important and useful than summative assessment. There are two reasons for this:

- First, it allows you to experience the OSCE process prior to the high stakes summative exam. Some students find the presence of an observer is sufficient enough to raise their anxiety levels so that their level of performance is adversely affected. On the other hand, some students find that the presence of an observer can enhance their performance.
- Second, until you have gone through this experience, you will not know how you are going to react and feel, and therefore how you are going to perform. So this 'dry run' will help you to think about how you will prepare and cope with the summative exam.

Summative OSCE assessments

Summative assessments typically come at the end of the course/module or section of learning and you will be awarded a final mark or grade for this section. This information will be used to inform you and the course leaders about your current abilities. You should be aware of what the pass mark is prior to the OSCE and the consequences of not achieving this. For example, it may mean that you have to resit the exam or it may mean that you cannot progress further in your course until you have passed this exam. If you are required in your course to be able to safely undertake a skill prior to commencing a practice placement, you may not be allowed to undertake your placement if you fail. Chapter 7 discusses what you should do after your formative or summative OSCE.

> Summative OSCEs usually come at the end of a period of study or module and may contribute to your final course mark.

Chapter 3 provides a range of practical tips and advice on what you need to do in order to be successful in your OSCE. You will also be able to assess your own learning style, which will help you to achieve better results in the long term.

Chapter summary

Skills teaching, simulated learning and OSCEs:

1   Are a rigorous way to identify your strengths and limitations.

2   Will enable you to demonstrate your knowledge, skills and attitude in real-life health care situations.

3   Can be undertaken in a clinical skills laboratory, computer-generated program or classroom.

4   Will enable you to work through scenarios.

5   Can give you instant feedback.

6   Are well researched as a validated method of assessment.

7   Allow you to practise and be examined in a safe environment.

8   Are time-limited.

9   Have quality assurance mechanisms built in.

10 Will help you to be a more competent professional learning in and from practice.

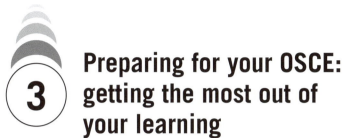

Preparing for your OSCE: getting the most out of your learning

3

Learning is not attained by chance; it must be sought for with ardour and attended to with diligence.

Abigail Adams (1744–1818)

By the end of this chapter you will:

○ Be able to understand your own learning style.
○ Be aware of the support available for students with disabilities including dyslexia and other specific learning difficulties.
○ Be able to understand the written information you may be given in preparation for your OSCE.
○ Have a range of practical tips and advice on what is being looked for in an exemplar OSCE.

This chapter will largely be dedicated to an annotated OSCE guide, similar to the one you may be given by your own tutor. The purpose of this is to demonstrate to you how to use this information to its full potential in your OSCE preparation. First, this chapter will look at learning styles in order to help you identify what type of learner you are and how this can affect your preparation for and performance in the OSCE.

Understanding your own learning style

There are lots of different learning styles that you will come across when you read further, such as auditory, visual and kinaesthetic, or extroverted and introverted. It is important to find a style that suits you rather than trying fit yourself into a style.

There is a range of learning style questionnaires to help you to:

- understand your own learning style;
- recognize the impact that your learning style has on your preparation and performance;
- tailor your preparation to your needs;
- get the best out of your preparation.

The following links take you to some of the most recognized questionnaires available online:

www.vark-learn.com/english/page.asp?p=questionnaire

and

www.learning-styles-online.com/

Knowing your learning style will make your learning more efficient. Table 3.1 is an example of a learning style questionnaire to ascertain your typical learning style, and the purpose is to get you to think about the way you learn and give you some tips on how to get the most from your learning. There is no 'good' or 'bad' style and you may find that you are a mixture of the four styles used in the example below. You may also find that there are areas you can develop from all four sections – do not worry if this is the case, it is perfectly normal.

In order to use the questionnaire you need to place ticks in the boxes next to the statements that you feel most apply to you. Once you have completed the questionnaire, see which section you have most ticks in and then look through the areas for development within that category. For example, if you have placed most of your ticks in the category entitled 'the jumper', use those study tips and areas for development. After you have identified your main style you can use this information to help you to revise more effectively.

Table 3.1 Learning styles questionnaire

	Tick	Study tips and areas for development
'The jumper'		
You dive in and have a go at things		• Aim to plan more and try reflection • Try stretching your mind to think more broadly and creatively • Consider a variety of alternatives before making a decision • Try listening to peers • Try to increase your interest so that you maintain your concentration for longer
You would rather get things over with quickly and not delay		
You are interested to see if things work		
You want to get on to the next task quickly		
You prefer short bouts of activity		
Total		
'The day-dreamer'		
You think a great deal about what you are doing		• Try to keep to your timings and once you've organized your work, stick to your plan • Set yourself priorities and action them • Take decisions rather than procrastinating • Try to be assertive and aim to take a few more risks
You like to look into things very thoroughly		
You delay getting started on things such as revision or writing		
Time just seems to pass quickly without you noticing		
You take time to do a time planner but like to rewrite it often as well		
Total		
'The rationalist'		
You prefer it if things make sense to you		• Try to take time to be reflective • Aim to work with others rather than trying to do everything yourself • Try to be accommodating of others' styles; they may not all be as organized as you • Aim to be more creative in your thinking
You like an explanation for things		
You tend to be very organized in whatever you do		
You like to solve very complicated problems		
You like things to be perfect once you've done them		
Total		

'The explorer'		
You find an interest in everything		
You have the ability to see the bigger picture		• Try to set goals and priorities
You know about lots of things		• Aim to take time to analyse things and think more critically
You want to know lots of details but don't often remember them		• Try to categorize things
You are so interested in things you aren't sure what is the main priority		• Aim to develop your memory for smaller details
Total		

Advice for students with disabilities including dyslexia and other specific learning difficulties

This section will provide any student who has disclosed a disability, dyslexia or other specific learning difficulty, with guidance on the type of adaptations/support they can expect to receive. An important factor to enable university staff to be able to support you appropriately is your need to *disclose* your disability to the relevant department/staff.

In 2001 the Special Educational Needs and Disability Act 2001 (SENDA) extended the Disability Discrimination Act 1995 (DDA) to cover post-16 education and introduced the need for a more proactive approach to anticipating and responding to the needs of students with a disability.

To ensure students with a disability have equal access to teaching and learning opportunities and appropriate support, every university will have a disability support department. This will have specially trained staff to help you identify the support or adjustments you require in order to perform your best in your OSCE. Disability services also work closely with the university staff to ensure that everything is put into place.

> Declare your disability as early as possible to gain maximum support and help.

If you don't declare your disability, these adjustments cannot be made. The legislation covering reasonable adjustments is considered in the light of the professional requirements of the health and social care qualification that you are undertaking. We need to carry out continuing risk assessments to ensure that you and/or the patients are not put at risk.

The following case study is an example of the type of support you might expect to get if you were a student studying with a disability.

Case study: support for a student with a disability

Carrie, a student with dyslexia, had met with the university student disability service to discuss, explore and put together detailed information about how lecturers could best support her in the teaching, learning and work placement environments.

Once Carrie and her disabled student adviser had agreed on a support plan, the information was distributed to module/course leaders to provide information on how best to support her.

For exams, Carrie would be given information in alternative formats and extra time allowed for reading and documentation during the OSCE.

The rest of this section will look in more detail at one of the commonest forms of learning disability – dyslexia.

Dyslexia

If you are assessed and registered as having dyslexia, you can expect the following adjustments for your OSCE. As a student with dyslexia you should also make use of your own university student disability service to ensure they notify module/course leaders how they can best support you in your learning. Every student with dyslexia will have different strategies to aid their learning and overcome their disability. It is therefore very important that you ensure that you communicate how you do this with your tutors.

Talk to your tutors about how you manage your disability.

SENDA requires HEIs to provide reasonable adjustments to enable disabled students, including dyslexic learners, to access the curriculum. It also states that an institution should not treat a disabled person *less favourably* than others for a reason that relates to their disability without justification.

If the student is at a *substantial disadvantage* the educational provider is required to make *reasonable adjustments*. The Quality Assurance Agency (QAA)

Code of Practice for the Assurance of Academic Quality and Standards in Higher Education (1999) confirms that: 'Assessment and examination policies, practices and procedures should provide disabled students with the same opportunity as their peers to demonstrate the achievement of learning outcomes' (Section 3, Precept 13).

Possible additional provisions include: computer; scribe (to write your dictation); reader (to read out questions and answers to you as required); individual room.

Recommendations by the Singleton Report, *Dyslexia in Higher Education* (1999) supported the view that academic staff should discount as far as possible errors in spelling, grammar and punctuation in dyslexic students' work, and that marking instead should be based on content, ideas and critical acumen.

A principle of SENDA is that any accommodation made for the dyslexic candidate should not undermine academic standards. For example, learning outcomes should not be compromised even though the process of assessment may differ. In many cases, reasonable adjustments may reflect good practice for all students.

While taking into account that these assessments may vary in format, the assumption is that they will comprise five main elements for which appropriate reasonable adjustments are made and these are shown in Table 3.2.

> There is lots of help available to support you if you have dyslexia or other specific learning disability.

Information you will receive prior to your OSCE

In order to help you prepare for your OSCE and to aid communication you should be provided with the following information from your academic staff. Ideally this should be given to you at the beginning of the semester in which your OSCE is going to take place. This will allow you plenty of time to prepare as you will know in detail what you are being assessed on. This information can be given to you in a number of ways, for example, in the course/module handbook, either electronically or as a paper copy, or as a presentation. Whichever format is used, you can expect to receive the following information:

- introduction to the OSCE;
- preparation for the OSCE;
- the OSCE examination itself (what you will be assessed on and how);
- the OSCE examination timings (when the OSCE will take place, how long you will have to complete the exam);

Table 3.2 Possible reasonable adjustments

Possible reasonable adjustments	A text to read	An activity	Information to be documented in patient records	An assessment interview	A written justification of action
25% extra time to read and process the written information	√		√		√
Use of a reader where appropriate	√				
Use of a pen and paper to take notes and/or highlighter pen	√				
Information presented on a range of coloured paper and using Arial/Century Gothic or Verdana fonts (recommended minimum 12pt)	√				
Provision of laptop for writing up notes			√		√
Provision of coloured paper			√		√
Blue marking cards to indicate the work is that of a dyslexic/ specific learning disabilities student			√		√

- the OSCE scenario/station;
- the OSCE checklist;
- the OSCE mark sheet;
- access to typical resources you will be using, such as documentation;
- related theory such as anatomy and physiology that may help you succeed in the exam;
- some tips on how to be successful in your exam.

Pre-reading

Even though a major part of the OSCE will be assessing your performance of a skill, you will also be assessed on your attitude and knowledge. Therefore it is essential that you have a good understanding of the theory behind the skill. The following list will give you some ideas of which resources you should utilize to support your pre-reading:

- reading lists from your course/module handbooks as these will highlight key texts and other resources that may have relevant information in order for you to gain the key knowledge, skills and attitude required for safe practice;
- OSCE checklists, which will have criteria related to the knowledge, skills and attitude against which you will be assessed;
- OSCE marking criteria, which will help you determine what level you are required to perform at to receive certain grades.

> Remember your OSCE is about knowledge, skills and attitude and you will ned to demonstrate competency in all of these areas.

Sample OSCE information sheet

Below you will find an example of the type of written information you could receive from your university to help prepare for your OSCE. The information has been supplemented with written text by us, designed to help you gain a greater understanding and be able to use the information to inform your preparation. The normal type is what you will receive from the university and *italic type* is the explanatory text that we have added.

Introduction to the Observed Structured Clinical Examination (OSCE)

An OSCE is a key component of the assessment strategy for module X. As a registered nurse you are personally accountable for ensuring your patient receives safe and competent care (NMC 2008a), therefore, the ability to perform clinical procedures with skill and confidence is essential.

This paragraph is setting the context and identifying the link that the OSCE has with the NMC's code of conduct, standards for proficiency and ESCs. Success in the OSCE will contribute to the requirements of your course.

An OSCE allows us to assess more than just knowledge. During the examination process the assessor is able to observe the following skills:

- interpersonal and communication skills;
- technical skills;
- observational skills;
- interpretation of data;
- documentation skills;
- initiative.

This list gives you guidance on what the examiner is looking for. It is clear that you are not just going to be assessed on a clinical skill but also on:

- *the way you interact and communicate with the patient;*
- *your ability to be able to perform the technical skills;*
- *your ability to observe and interpret the data.*

Imagine you are applying the above list to recording a patient's respiratory rate. The examiner is not only assessing whether you have the technical skill of being able to count your patient's respiratory rate (technical skills) but that you have the ability to ascertain if their breathing is regular, symmetrical and effortless and that the rate is within the normal limits (observational skills and ability to interpret data). An example of this could be undertaking an OSCE with an 8-year-old child. The normal respiration rate range for a 5–8-year-old child is 15–25 with an average of 20. If during your OSCE the respiratory rate of the 8-year-old child you are examining is 28, you would need to inform the examiner and parent or carer that this reading is slightly higher than normal. To demonstrate that you have a true understanding you would need to highlight to the examiner what you consider to be the normal range for this particular patient (as this may be normal for them). You need to consider whether there has been any recent events that could have caused the increase, for example, has the child just run down the corridor, or recently been crying, which could cause an increase in their respiratory rate. You need to state what you are going to do about this; a typical response would be that an increase in respiratory rate in isolation is unlikely to be anything significant. In this case you would need to consider the other observations and state that you would report this to your mentor or a senior member of staff.

You will then need to document your findings accurately, ensuring that the documentation meets the standards prescribed by the NMC (documentation skills). In respect to initiative, the examiner is assessing your ability to act appropriately during the scenario, as mentioned above.

The OSCE also allows for self-evaluation through video-recording and constructive feedback, and promotes student confidence.

This tells you that the OSCE is going to be recorded and you can expect feedback from the examiners, but you should also use the experience to carry out a self-evaluation. Chapter 7 gives you further guidance on how to make the most out of the feedback you receive during and following your OSCE.

Preparation for the OSCE

The OSCE examinations will be held in the skills centres at your campus. Please refer to your module timetable on the virtual learning environment for this module for the week/days that have been allocated for these examinations. Notification of the specific date and time of your examination will be displayed two weeks prior to the week that the exams are being held.

This tells you about the venue for the OSCE and where you need to go to find out the exact date and time of your exam. It is therefore your responsibility to follow this up. If you fail to turn up for the OSCE, as you have not found out this information, the consequence could be failing the module or even being asked to leave the course.

Please bring the following to your OSCE exam:

- ID badge with photo and student number;
- watch with second hand;
- pens as required;
- full uniform as per uniform policy.

The above list is to ensure that you have everything you need to perform in the OSCE. It tells you that the university will provide any other equipment that might be required in the OSCE. A note of caution, however: if you fail to have your university identification badge with you and your OSCE is a summative exam, many universities will not allow you to go ahead, so this really is an essential item not to forget!

The OSCE examination

Please arrive for your OSCE at least five minutes before your allocated exam time. Upon arrival report to the designated room and please have your student ID badge ready to be checked.

Universities have very strict regulations about examinations and entering after the exam has started is usually forbidden. Therefore, if you are late and unable to commence your OSCE this is often counted as a 'non-submission'. Once again, depending on the type of assessment, the consequences of this could be extreme. Therefore you should plan your journey to the university very carefully to ensure that you arrive in adequate time. However, do not go to the designated room until your allocated time. This is for two reasons:

- *first, you do not want to block the surrounding area as you will often not be allowed in early, as students who are being examined before you will still be there;*
- *second, it could increase your nerves!*

As mentioned earlier, you may not be able to enter the OSCE without your student ID badge, so do not presume that the person checking you in will know you; this may not be the case. Universities often bring in extra staff during exams to help run them smoothly.

You will then be given 10 minutes to prepare for your OSCE. During this time you will be given a copy of the OSCE scenario, and an OSCE checklist for you to read.

This informs you that you will have some time prior to entering the examination to remind you of what is required during the OSCE. If you have left it until this time to ascertain what is required of you it is unlikely that you will perform well in the exam! However, if the OSCE is assessing a number of skills at different stations it is here that you are told which stations/ skills you will be assessed on. This 10 minutes is very useful as a short, quiet and reflective period before you enter the exam. Chapter 5 expands on how to cope with pre-OSCE nerves.

The OSCE checklist is once again just a reminder and you should have studied this is great detail prior to arriving at the exam. Below is an example checklist that we have annotated to help you ascertain what the examiner is looking for.

At the end of 10 minutes you will be escorted to the simulation ward X and directed to the corresponding patient's bed space.

This informs you where the actual OSCE will take place and indicates that there will be a number of stations running simultaneously.

You will have 15 minutes in total for the examination. During this time you will be asked to complete three out of a possible four procedures. You need to complete all three procedures to be in a position to gain a pass in the OSCE.

You have 15 minutes to complete three out of the possible four procedures listed. This time allowance will help you with your practice and rehearsing. When you are practising the skills and as you get more confident and proficient in them, you will need to ensure that you can fit different combinations of the procedures into 15 minutes. It is very clear from the above statement that not only do you have to meet the requirements on the OSCE checklist but you also have to complete the task. This is not always the case for some OSCEs, where you may only have to complete certain aspects before the examiner is able to assess you. It is important that you ask the leader of your OSCEs what happens if you do not complete in the allocated time if this is not explicit in the information given to you.

The possible procedures are as follows:

Adult/mental health/learning disability fields

- Temperature measurement
- Pulse rate measurement
- Respiratory rate measurement
- Blood pressure measurement

Child field

- Temperature measurement
- Pulse rate measurement

- Respiratory rate measurement
- Apex beat measurement

The above lists are informing you about which clinical skills you are being assessed on. The usual reason why you are not being assessed on them all is due to time and resources. However, the fact that you are not aware of which you will be assessed on until you report to the OSCE means that you still need to learn all four procedures.

To ensure you are fully prepared, you need to utilize the learning opportunities provided by the university and clinical practice. You will never be assessed on anything that you have not been taught. When the assessment is an OSCE, you are usually taught the skills during simulated learning in the simulated learning environment for the practical element. However, the related knowledge/theory may well be gained via a lecture/ seminar or recommended reading. It is therefore essential that you attend all of these sessions, otherwise you may miss not only the practice time but also the demonstration and other important information such as related knowledge, and what is expected of you in the OSCE.

Following the initial session, most universities will facilitate further practice sessions nearer the time of the exam. Make sure you are aware when and where these are taking place. If your OSCE is summative you will be given the opportunity of a formative OSCE. This is invaluable, not only because of the feedback you will be given, but also because it will give you the opportunity to experience what it is like being watched so closely. Chapter 2 discusses the difference between formative and summative OSCEs while Chapter 7 discusses types of feedback in greater detail and gives you advice on how to act upon your feedback.

Self-assessment and peer assessment can also help you prepare and succeed in your OSCE. Universities will often have an independent skills laboratory where students can go either individually or in groups to practise clinical skills. However, remember you are not doing yourself or your peers any favours by saying they did well if they did not and vice versa! Therefore constructive criticism is essential.

Clinical practice offers essential opportunities to prepare for your OSCEs. Share as much information as possible with your mentor so they can help you with your preparation. Ask them to use the OSCE checklist provided by the university to assess you whenever you carry out the activities on which you are going to be examined.

You need to use every opportunity to practise the skills required: this could be supervised practice in the clinical area with your mentor, or in

> the simulated learning environment with university staff, or self-directed. Students have found that the more confident and competent they are with the skills prior to entering the exam, the better they do.
>
> Even though a major part of the OSCE will be assessing your performance of a skill, you will be assessed on other aspects such as related knowledge/theory, as discussed previously. It is therefore essential that you have a good understanding of the theory behind a skill. You should use the reading lists from your course/module handbooks as these will highlight key texts and other resources that may have relevant information.
>
> As well as the OSCE checklist, if an OSCE is being graded and is not just a pass/fail, there will be a marking criteria sheet attached. This is another valuable source of information as it will have criteria related to knowledge, skills and attitude. This will not only give you pointers as to what components will be tested but you can ascertain at what level you are required to perform to receive certain grades. For example, in order to obtain an A grade or distinction under the knowledge section of a physical assessment OSCE, you will need to: 'Demonstrate a detailed and accurate knowledge of key aspects of relevant underpinning theory. Confidently discriminate between normal and abnormal findings.' Therefore, not only do you need to be able to carry out the physical assessment, you need also to have a wide depth of knowledge of pathology; hence, gaining access to physiology texts is essential.

In all instances you will be expected to accurately and correctly document your findings on the charts provided.

> Concise and accurate documentation of any care that you have given, including taking observations, should be a recorded in the patient's notes. The following statements from the NMC code of conduct for nurses and midwives (2008) set the standards and this is what you will be assessed against. The sections that are relevant to this OSCE are in bold type to help you pick them out.

The examination timekeeper will alert you when you have five minutes of the exam time remaining.

> The rationale for this is to give you an indication if you need to speed up at all. For example, if you have taken 10 minutes to only complete one of the skills being assessed and you have two further skills to complete, you risk of running out of time. However, if you are on your last skill you may feel you can slow down a bit and try and improve your OSCE by providing further information to the examiner about what you are doing, or providing greater explanation to the patient.

Once the 15 minutes has elapsed the timekeeper will announce the end of the examination and you will be escorted from the examination room.

Even if you finish your OSCE prior to the 15 minutes you will not be able to leave the room. The reason for this is so that you do not disturb any student who has not completed. If you do finish the OSCE early, you should sit down and go through the process in your head to ensure you have completed everything you were required to do, including rechecking any documentation you have completed. It may be that even if you say you have finished your OSCE, you suddenly remember something that you should have done, and as long as you complete it within the 15 minutes you can continue. For example, if you forgot to inform the patient if their observations were within the normal ranges you could do this; however, you will probably be marked down as your OSCE performance would not have been fluent. On the other hand, if this is one of the essential criteria it is better that you gain a lower mark than fail.

A quality assurance person and timekeeper will be present during the OSCE. They will not be examining you but observing the examination process.

This is a quality assurance process to ensure that every student is being assessed equally. This information is provided to make you aware that there will be more people in the examination room than just the examiners.

All OSCE assessments will be video-recorded using SMOTS.

This informs you that the OSCE will be recorded using a video-recording system that the university has in place. Your university may utilize another system of recording the OSCE, so ensure that you are aware of this system. The recording of the OSCE is for quality assurance purposes and also to help you reflect upon the process. It does not matter if you pass or fail the OSCE; viewing and reflecting on your performance will help you develop further. Reflective practice is discussed further in Chapter 7.

The OSCE scenario

'Your patient is in hospital for tests and I would like you to perform the following procedures (you will be told to perform three out of the following four procedures, temperature, pulse, respirations or blood pressure). Please document all measurements on the observation chart provided. Please explain to the patient whether their observations are within the School of Health and Social Care recommended normal range for that individual.'

This scenario is very explicit and as soon as you have received this written information you can start to prepare for your OSCE. It informs you that:

- *your patient is in a hospital setting;*
- *why they are there;*
- *what you are expected to do.*

When you receive a scenario, ensure you break it down and highlight the key aspects to help with your preparation. In the above scenario the key aspects are the skills you will be assessed on and the fact that you not only have to take and interpret the observations but you also need to document them on the observation chart provided.

Every clinical area has slightly different documentation, so ensure you get a copy of the documentation you will be expected to use. You can then become familiar with it and the OSCE will not be the first time you have seen it. If it is not provided, ask for sample documentation so that you can see what you are expected to do. A sample OSCE checklist is provided on page 67, completed to the standard required in order to pass the OSCE. You are asked to explain to the patient if the patient's observations are within the normal range of that individual. This is where the tutors are assessing your knowledge base and whether you can interpret the observations that you have taken and take appropriate action.

OSCE 'top tips'

Taking a patient's temperature

Ensure you insert the tympanic thermometer probe into the ear nearest to you. If you need to record the temperature in the other ear because you are worried the reading was not accurate (e.g. presence of ear wax), then make sure you walk around the bed/chair and approach the patient from the other side.

Ensure you place the tympanic thermometer probe carefully into the ear canal and make sure you angle the probe towards the patient's nose to ensure you are not taking a reading from the skin of the ear canals. Incorrect insertion can lead to an inaccurate reading.

Taking a patient's pulse

When taking the patient's pulse, the rhythm and amplitude should be assessed as well as the rate.

Taking a patient's respirations

The patient may alter their breathing rate if they are aware their respirations are being counted. You can reduce this risk by pretending to count the pulse but instead count the patient's respiration rate. If you need to stop to write the respiratory rate down on a piece of paper or your observation chart then you can always ask the patient if you can take their pulse again.

If you have difficulty seeing the rise and fall of the patient's chest then it may be helpful to ask them to place their arm across their chest. However, this may increase their awareness that their respirations are being counted and alter their breathing rate.

Taking a patient's blood pressure

If the blood pressure cuff 'blows up' while you are inflating it or you hear a 'ripping' sound, you have probably put the cuff on inside out. Take it off and turn it the right way. You should be able to read the writing on the cuff. You can then start the procedure again.

If you cannot hear the blood pressure, check you have inserted the stethoscope ear pieces into your ears correctly. They should be angled towards your nose. If you have inserted the ear pieces correctly, you should hear a 'drum' sound when you tap the diaphragm (flat end) of the stethoscope. If you cannot hear this sound, turn the stethoscope around so that the ear pieces fit in the other way, then tap the diaphragm of the stethoscope again.

Make sure the end of the stethoscope is turned so that the hole is not visible when you look at the bell side.

Common mistakes when taking a patient's blood pressure include:

- the patient is talking while you are taking the blood pressure – this can cause an increase in the systolic pressure by up to 17mmHg;
- failing to support the arm in the correct position;
- failing to complete the radial check to establish the approximate systolic pressure;
- deflating the cuff too fast or too slow;
- failing to record the diastolic reading at the disappearance of the Korotkoff sound (Phase V).

Documentation

Make sure you complete your patient's full name (surname and first name) and hospital number on the observation chart, along with the year, date/month and time.

Take care to record your readings accurately on the observation chart. Make sure your recordings are all on the same line and place dots/crosses, etc. in the middle of the box *not* on the vertical lines.

If you need to make an alteration, make sure these are dated, timed and signed. Please see the observation chart on page 67 for an example of how observations should be correctly documented.

And finally...

Make sure you read the OSCE checklist carefully. All items in **bold** on the checklist must have been demonstrated in order to pass the OSCE.

> *The above sections are just some top tips/reminders to help you succeed in your OSCE. Do not forget that the examiners want you to succeed! These tips may not always be provided in a written format but may be via a presentation given during a lecture/seminar/simulated session, or by electronic means. These tips have normally been developed utilizing the examiners' experiences of previous OSCEs – for example, what have been found to be the common mistakes that students make.*

The checklist below informs you about what you are required to do in order to pass the OSCE. We have annotated it to help you identify what the examiners are looking for. It is hoped that you can then apply the same principles to the OSCE checklist that has been provided by your university.

Physiological measurement OSCE checklist

EXAMINER'S NAME ....
STUDENT LABEL ....
STATION ....
DATE ....

Achievement of a pass grade requires all components in bold to be demonstrated as a minimum.

> *This is a very important statement; it provides you with what the minimum requirement is for you to pass the OSCE. If you do not achieve one or more*

bold item you will automatically fail even if you achieve the rest of the OSCE perfectly. You may feel this is a bit harsh, however, the rationale is that without achieving any of the bold items to the standard set in the statement, you have either breached professional standards, or carried out practice unsafely. By achieving all of the bold items to the required standard you will pass the OSCE. In addition, if you complete the non-bold items you will pass the OSCE with a higher mark/level of performance. You should never aim to just pass!

Table 3.3 Physiological measurement OSCE checklist

Activity	Performance expected
Professional behaviour	☐ **Behaves in a professional manner consistent with professional standards** ↑ *You need to refer to the NMC Code (2008a) to ascertain what these professional standards are.* ☐ **Performs the activity with due respect to patient safety, privacy and dignity** ↑ *This relates once again to the NMC Code (2008a) but also the NMC ESC and standards of proficiency (2007a, 2007b).* ☐ Adheres to the school professional dress code ↑ *This tells you that you are expected to complete the OSCE in your uniform. This may be a clinical uniform or simulated practice uniform.* ☐ Introduces themselves to patient/client/carer giving name and status ☐ Asks what the patient/client/carer would like to be called
Communication skills	☐ **Checks patient identity verbally, and against the patient's/ client's ID bracelet** ☐ Clearly explains all of the procedures to the patient/ client/carer using language appropriate to the patient/ client/carer ☐ Checks patient's/client's/carer's understanding of procedures

(Continued)

Activity	Performance expected
	☐ Offers clear answers to any questions the patient/client/carer may ask
	☐ **Gains the informed consent from the appropriate individual/s**
	☐ Verbally concludes the procedure and ensures the comfort of the patient/client/carer
	☐ Demonstrates appropriate positioning/body language/eye contact/use of touch while explaining/performing the procedures
	☐ Speaks clearly
	☐ Uses open-ended questions
	This section is assessing your communication skills. There are two elements that you are required to carry out as a minimum in order to pass the OSCE. These are requirements of the NMC Code (2008a) and in your preparation you need to ensure you fully understand what is required and why it is deemed essential in order to pass the OSCE. The remaining statements are also important; however, they do not make you unsafe by not completing them. If this OSCE was just assessing your communication skills they would be in bold.
	☐ Explains to the patient/client/carer the purpose of the procedure
Tympanic thermometer	☐ **Covers the speculum with disposable cover without contaminating it**
	☐ **Gently inserts into the ear canal, adjacent to but not touching tympanic membrane**
	☐ **Leaves thermometer in for correct amount of time – indicated by a bleeping sound**
	☐ **Removes thermometer without contaminating hands**
	☐ **Reads temperature accurately (within 0.5 degrees of examiner's reading)**
	Examiner's reading ....

Student's reading ....

Examiner's checked reading ....

☐ **Discards probe mindful of infection control risks**

☐ **Informs the patient/client/carer if the reading is within an acceptable range**

☐ **Informs the patient/client/carer of the normal ranges for temperature measurement for the client group as taught by the School of Health and Social Care**

☐ Replaces equipment appropriately

This section and the sections below are intended to inform you how you are expected to carry out the procedures that you have been asked to perform. You will be assessed against each of the statements and a tick or cross will be placed in a box next to the statement depending on whether you perform the action. If you attempt to perform an action and you either do this incorrectly or not to the required standard, a cross will be inserted into the box.

The order that the actions are listed in is usually the most coherent way of carrying out each of the skills; however, it is not always the only way. For example if you prefer to inform the patient about the normal ranges of temperature at the beginning of the OSCE this will not affect the outcome.

Pulse rate recording

☐ Explains to the patient/client/carer the purpose of the procedure

☐ Checks for recent exercise

☐ Checks that the patient's arm is resting comfortably

☐ **Locates radial pulse accurately**

☐ **Using watch with second hand and counts for 60 seconds**

☐ **Heart rate noted correctly (within 6 of the examiner's reading)**

(Continued)

Activity	Performance expected
	Examiner's reading ....
	Student's reading ....
	Examiner's checked reading ....
	☐ **Informs the patient/client/carer if the reading is within an acceptable range**
	☐ **Informs the patient/client/carer of the normal ranges for temperature measurement for the client group as taught by the School of Health and Social Care**
	▲ *When recording the patient's pulse, checking for recent exercise is an example of best practice, but not asking the patient this question will not make you unsafe. The rationale for asking this question is related to you understanding that recent exercise can increase the pulse rate. If you do ask such questions, it is advisable to explain to either the patient or the examiner why you have asked that question. This will show the examiner that you have not just memorized the checklist but have an understanding of why that element of the assessment is important.*
Respiratory rate recording	☐ Explains to the patient/client/carer the purpose of the procedure
	☐ Checks for recent exercise
	☐ **Observes/feels/ listens for respirations for 60 seconds**
	☐ **Respiratory rate noted correctly (within 2 of the examiner's reading)**
	Examiner's reading ....
	Student's reading ....
	Examiner's checked reading ....
	☐ **Informs the patient/client/carer if the reading is within an acceptable range**
	☐ **Informs the patient/client/carer of the normal ranges for temperature measurement for the client group as taught by the School of Health and Social Care**

	If any of the statements conflict with what you have seen in practice or read in the literature, you need to question the statement to increase your knowledge base. For example, until recently it was documented and common practice that if a respiratory rate or pulse rate was regular you need only to observe/feel for 30 seconds and then double your reading. However, more recent evidence suggests that it should be observed/felt for 1 minute.
Blood pressure recording	☐ Explains to the patient/client/carer the purpose of the procedure
	☐ Checks for recent exercise
	☐ **Ensures that tight or restrictive clothing is removed from the arm**
	☐ **Ensures the patient's arm is well supported at the patient's heart level with the palm of the hand facing upwards**
	☐ **Cuff size selected – i.e. cuff covers 80% of the circumference of the upper arm**
	☐ **Brachial pulse palpated and the centre of the bladder placed over it**
	☐ **Bottom edge of cuff placed about 2.5cm above the ante-cubital fosse**
	☐ Cuff applied firmly but not too tightly
	☐ Radial pulse palpated and cuff inflated until pulse disappears; cuff deflated immediately
	☐ States estimated systolic pressure
	☐ Stethoscope ear pieces inserted into ears correctly
	☐ **Brachial pulse palpated and stethoscope placed directly over it**
	☐ Cuff inflated to 20–30mmHg above the stated estimated systolic
	☐ **Cuff deflated at an approximate rate of 2–4mmHg per second**
	☐ Promptly releases cuff at the end of the procedure

(Continued)

Activity	Performance expected
	☐ **Systolic and diastolic pressures correctly noted (student's systolic reading to be within + or – 10mmHg of the examiner's systolic reading and student's diastolic reading to be within + or – 6mmHg of examiner's diastolic reading)** Examiner's reading.. Student's reading... Examiner's checked reading.......................... ☐ **Informs the patient/client/carer if the reading is within an acceptable range** ☐ **Informs the patient/client/carer of the normal ranges for temperature measurement for the client as taught by the School of Health and Social Care** ☐ Stethoscope ear pieces cleaned with an alcohol wipe ☐ Clothing replaced and patient left comfortable ▲ *This section provides you with the procedure for reading a blood pressure. You are expected in all the procedures to inform the patient/carer if their readings are within an acceptable range for them (therefore taking into account their age and any pathology they may have), and also if they are within the normal range. This is assessing your knowledge base and informs you that you need to have a certain level of knowledge related to the skills you are performing in order to pass this OSCE.*
Apex beat (to be carried out on sim newby or sim baby)	☐ Explains to the patient/client/carer the purpose of the procedure ☐ Checks the stethoscope is working and set to use the diaphragm ☐ **Places the diaphragm of the stethoscope in the correct position for the child's age** (fourth intercostal space slightly left of nipple line for children under 7 years/ fifth intercostal space, below nipple for children over 7 years) ☐ **Uses watch with second hand to count apical pulse for 60 seconds**

	☐ **Heart rate noted correctly (within 6 of the pre-set reading)**
	Pre-set reading............................
	Student's reading........................
	☐ **Informs the patient/client/carer if the reading is within an acceptable range with reference to child/infant's level of activity** (e.g. sleeping/crying); articulates how levels of activity might influence this
	☐ **Informs the patient/client/carer of the normal ranges for child/infant's age as taught by the School of Health and Social Care**
	☐ Stethoscope ear pieces cleaned with an alcohol wipe
	☐ Clothing replaced and patient left comfortable; well-being of patient ascertained
	This section demonstrates how you need to find and listen to the apex beat. It also clearly states that you will be carrying out this skill on a manikin (sim newby or sim baby). Therefore you should ensure you have practised using such a manikin.
Documentation	☐ **Patient's full name and hospital number clearly written on the observation chart and can be easily read by others**
	☐ **All observations are dated (date, month and year) and timed**
	☐ **All observations are charted accurately**
	☐ **All alterations or additions are dated, timed and signed**
	☐ **The record is written in black ink**
	This section states how you need to record your observations on the observation chart provided. There is an example of an observation chart on page 67 to help you apply this. You will see that all elements are bold, because all criteria are set by the NMC.

(Continued)

Activity	Performance expected
PASS/REFERRAL Feedback	This section will be used by the examiner to indicate if you have passed the OSCE or have been referred (need to resit or retake the OSCE). It informs you that you will not be given a mark for this OSCE, just a pass or referral. In Chapter 6 we have provided you with an example of an OSCE showing that after each statement you can gain a score. The scores are added up and then converted into a percentage and grade. There is also an example of an OSCE which includes a checklist not dissimilar to this one, but is converted into a percentage by utilizing marking criteria. This section will also give you feedback as to how you can improve. Please refer to Chapter 7 where feedback is discussed in greater detail.

The checklists are one of the most valuable pieces of information in helping you prepare for your OSCE. As mentioned previously, not only does the checklist inform you of what you will be expected to do in order to pass the OSCE, it gives you an indication of the standard that is expected of you. This will vary depending on where you are in your training. For example, the amount of knowledge this OSCE is expecting you to have in relation to interpreting your findings is minimal. You need only know if they are within normal ranges and be aware of those normal ranges, so this exam could be taken very early in your training. However, if you were asked to carry out the same OSCE towards the end of your training, you would probably be expected to explain how abnormal pathology would affect observations – for example, what would increase a patient's blood pressure, or why infection causes pyrexia.

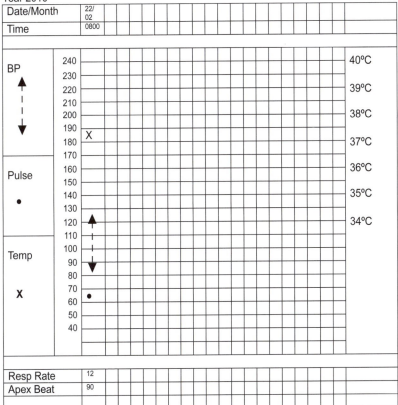

OBSERVATION CHART	HOSPITAL NUMBER...07984365......................................
	SURNAME.....Smith...
	FIRST NAMES.......Suzy...

PLEASE RECORD YOUR OBSERVATIONS FROM LEFT TO RIGHT

Year 2010

Date/Month	22/ 02																			
Time	0800																			

| BP ↕ Pulse • Temp X | 240 230 220 210 200 190 180 170 160 150 140 130 120 110 100 90 80 70 60 50 40 | X ↑ ⁞ ↓ • | | | | | | | | | | | | | | | | 40°C 39°C 38°C 37°C 36°C 35°C 34°C |

Resp Rate	12																
Apex Beat	90																

Diagram 3.1 Observation chart

↑ *This is informing you how you are expected to record the observations and gives you an example of the documentation that you may be using.*

We hope that you have found the sample OSCE information that we have annotated for you useful. What we suggest you do is, once you receive this type of information from your tutors, make notes not dissimilar to ours in order to help you start your preparation. This important task will help you ascertain:

• which clinical skills you are required to perform during your OSCE;
• the level of knowledge and skills you need to display;
• any queries or questions you may have, early on, so you can get the answers.

Chapter 4 will help you to understand the expected layout of the room for your OSCE and the types of simulated clients/models or manikins that will be used during your OSCE. You will learn to recognize the role and behaviour of your assessors/examiners and be aware of the role-behaviour and performance required by you in order to prepare for your OSCE.

Chapter summary

1 Ensure you take every opportunity possible to undergo supervised simulated practice so that you get used to the environment and equipment that will be used in your exam.

2 Attend formative OSCEs and act upon the feedback that the examiners give you.

3 Ensure you have the adequate level of knowledge and skills to undertake the OSCE by making use of lecture notes and other resources.

4 Make use of any additional information the lecturers provide to help you succeed in your exam.

5 If you have a disability, ensure that the module/course leader is aware so that any reasonable adjustments can be made.

6 Aim to let your module/course leader know as early as possible if you have a disability.

7 Be sure about whether you are taking a *formative* or *summative* attempt.

8 Ensure you know how many attempts you are able to undertake.

9 Aim to work out your own learning style.

10 Identify which areas from your learning style analysis you can develop further.

What to expect from your OSCE

4

What we see depends mainly on what we look for.

John Lubbock (1834–1913)

> ## By the end of this chapter you will:
> ○ Understand the expected layout of the room for your OSCE.
> ○ Understand the types of simulated clients/models or manikins that will be used during your OSCE.
> ○ Recognize the role and behaviour of your assessors/examiners.
> ○ Be aware of the role-behaviour and performance required in order to prepare for your OSCE.
> ○ Understand the mechanisms used to ensure quality assurance (e.g. roaming moderator, cameras and external examiners).

The layout of the room

When you enter your examination the layout of the room should be fairly familiar to you, assuming you have undertaken simulated learning in a practice skills laboratory before. If not, the photographs throughout this chapter will give you an idea of what to expect.

Depending on the focus of the examination, it may take place in a computer room, skills laboratory, simulated ward, simulated home setting or classroom. The room may look slightly different to how you are used to seeing it, as there will probably be a series of examination stations set up. These stations may all be identical if you are all being tested on the same skills – for example, administration of medicines. Alternatively, there may be a number of different stations which you are required to rotate around, such as hand-washing, taking and recording vital signs and urinary catheterization.

Whichever format is used, each station will normally either be behind curtains or screened off. The reason for this is to give you privacy throughout your exam (see Photograph 1). All the equipment that you are required to use should be available at the station, other than those items that you have been asked to bring with you – for example, a pen and/or fob watch.

Photograph 1 shows you the layout of a room set up for several stations running simultaneously. You can see that each station is separated by curtains to ensure privacy for you and also to ensure that privacy and dignity can be maintained for your patient throughout the examination.

Equipment used

The equipment used in the OSCE will depend on the type of exam you are undertaking. You should be familiar with any equipment you are using during the OSCE – for example, observation recording equipment, documentation

Photograph 1 Bed stations with curtains

such as medication charts, and manikins. You should not be required to use any equipment that you have not been shown before or had the opportunity to practise using before the OSCE. Please remember that the university will give you the opportunity to practise using the equipment and if you do not take up this offer you cannot report in the OSCE that you have not used or seen this equipment before. This is an added reason why it is important that you take every opportunity offered to practise in the simulated learning environment.

Photograph 2 shows a student taking a patient's temperature. You can see she is using a tympanic thermometer. There are several different types of tympanic thermometer on the market, therefore different clinical areas may have different thermometers from the type that the university uses. Each thermometer works in a slightly different way and if you come across a piece of equipment in the OSCE that you are not familiar with, it could faze you and cause errors. However, not being used to the equipment is *not* a valid excuse for under-performing in an OSCE and it is expected, as a health care professional, that you are confident and competent in using any appropriate equipment to support the care that you give to your patients. Therefore, it is essential that you find out what equipment you will be using during the OSCE.

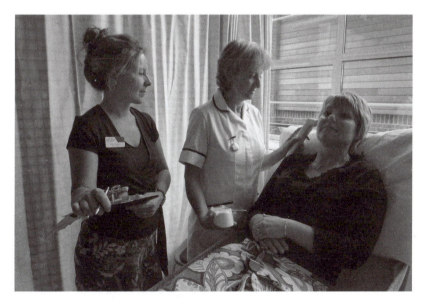

Photograph 2 Taking a temperature reading

> Ensure you are familiar with any equipment that you will be required to use in your OSCE.

Types of simulated client/model

This section details what is to be expected from the following simulated clients and the differences between them, as well as the varying approaches you will need to adopt.

The different types of simulated client you may come across are:

- members of the public, both adults and children;
- colleagues/peers;
- actors;
- practice staff;
- manikins.

With any live model in a simulated setting you need to ensure you adhere to the main professional principles that would guide you in your professional life. In particular, the ESC that states: 'treat them with dignity and respect them as individuals', which comes under the broad heading of 'care, compassion and communication'.

Confidentiality and ethics should guide your behaviour. You will also be adhering to the NMC standards for proficiency, and in particular: 'make the care of people your first concern, treating them as individuals and respecting their dignity'. Professional behaviour is just as important in a simulated learning environment as it is in a practice area and your behaviour should mirror this.

Your models may be used to acting as patients, or it may be their first time. Either way they will have been well prepared by the academic team as to their expected performance/behaviour during your OSCE. There are a range of live models that could be used as a simulated patient and they will now be discussed. However, the most important point for you to remember is whatever the type of live model or situation, you need to behave towards them as you would towards any patient you work with in your professional life.

To help you with your performance, and to avoid any nasty surprises before you turn up for your OSCE, you should find out who will be acting as your patient: will it be a professional actor, a volunteer, a fellow student or a tutor? Never presume who will be your patient – it may unnerve you if you were expecting a patient volunteer and when you are introduced to your patient you find that it is one of your tutors or a student from the university.

> Ensure you find out prior to the OSCE what type of simulated patient you will have to perform your OSCE on. Will it be a live model or a manikin, and if a live model, what type?

Members of the public, both adults and children

Members of the general public are often used as simulated clients for OSCEs. These people are volunteers who will either be paid a minimal sum and/or have their travel expenses paid. They are usually adults but may occasionally be children if specialist knowledge is required. These volunteers are often people who have been service users or carers of service users, or may be retired health and social care practitioners. Many volunteers will undertake the assessments on a regular basis and so will be well skilled in their roles.

All volunteers will undergo some formal training to ensure they perform consistently to the same level and act in the same manner. This ensures that no student is disadvantaged by a 'patient' asking more questions than required for the level of OSCE, or overacting their role. The key factor is that all students should have the same experience as each other when undertaking the OSCE.

However, there is a note of caution when your patient is a live model. Every patient is different and if you are asked to perform any kind of assessment on them – for example, taking and recording their blood pressure manually – it is very important that if you detect any observations which are outside the 'normal' range for that client group, you report your findings to the examiner. You also need to outline a potential action plan. This will form part of the OSCE and is your opportunity to demonstrate to the examiner your knowledge base and decision-making skills.

If the OSCE requires you to carry out any type of assessment, you will not be informing the volunteer or examiner of anything new, as it is good practice that all volunteers used in OSCEs will have a baseline assessment undertaken prior to you examining them. This will ensure that any abnormality will have been identified beforehand but will also give the examiner an indication of what the patient's examination results are so that when you assess and record them, they can see immediately if you have undertaken a correct assessment.

Example 1: a volunteer's experience of being a 'patient'

Molly is a retired nurse and enjoys participating in OSCEs. It gives her a chance to see what new practice is being taught and to see her fellow 'patients'. Today Molly is being an OSCE patient having vital signs recorded. When Molly arrives for the OSCE she is given instructions by the OSCE tutor about the OSCE for the session.

Molly is required to have her vital signs taken prior to the session so that a baseline is ascertained. Molly's observations are recorded by Abir, the OSCE examiner who is working with Molly for that session. Her observations are: BP 145/85, P 80, T 36.7, R 22.

Molly settles herself into the bed space area and awaits the first-year student, Becky. Becky is nervous but Molly tries to put her at ease by smiling at her and looking encouraging.

Abir checks that Becky understands what she has to do for the OSCE and runs through her role as tutor. Abir asks Molly to start when the bell sounds, indicating the start of the OSCE for all the students in that session.

Becky explains the procedure to Molly and takes her observations. Becky records the observations on the standard sheet. Following the end of the OSCE Abir compares the observations and finds that they are all the same except that Becky recorded the BP at 140/85. The tutor re-records Molly's BP and finds that it has dropped to 142/85 and so Becky's recording can be deemed accurate.

Becky will in particular have adhered to the following ESCs when undertaking this OSCE:

- 'treat them with dignity and respect them as individuals';
- 'ensure that their consent will be sought prior to care or treatment being given';
- 'ensure that their rights will be respected'.

Colleagues/peers

Your colleagues and peers may be used in simulated learning sessions as models that you can practise on and occasionally be examined on. If you are simulating a patient for one of your peers during their OSCE, you need to act in a professional manner and ensure you behave as if you were in a full examination setting. It is very important to remember that you are acting as a professional when undertaking an OSCE and as such you are required by the NMC Code to maintain confidentiality. This applies whether you are in a student role or acting as a model patient. You should not discuss the actions of the student with anyone except the examiner and *definitely not* with fellow students. However, acting as a patient for one of your peers is an excellent learning opportunity and can help you with your OSCE and clinical practice. Below is an example so you can see when and how you might be asked to act as a patient for your peers.

Example 2: students' experiences of undertaking an OSCE and being a 'patient'

Tom is a third-year mental health student and he is being a 'patient' for a formative OSCE for Sanjay, a second-year mental health student. Tom has undertaken this role before and finds it very rewarding to help fellow peers to improve their practice. The OSCE being examined on this occasion is 'administration of medicines'. Tom is given an information sheet by the OSCE tutor. This sheet details what type of patient Tom is to be for the session. In this case Tom is a 70-year-old man with depression and long-standing asthma.

Tom works with the OCSE tutor to make sure the bed space is set up correctly for the OSCE and is standard to all other bed spaces being used for OSCEs that day.

Tom participates in the OSCE and at the completion of it gives feedback to Sanjay with the OSCE examiner. He explains what it felt like to be a patient being treated by Sanjay and suggests how Sanjay could improve his practice.

The OSCE enabled Tom to practise the following ESCs:

- 'protect and treat as confidential all information relating to themselves and their care';

- 'respond appropriately to feedback from patients/clients, the public and a wide range of sources as a vehicle for learning and development';
- 'safely delegate care to others and respond appropriately when a task is delegated to them';
- 'safely lead, coordinate and manage care'.

This OSCE enabled Sanjay to practise the following ESCs:

- 'work within the legal and ethical framework that underpins safe and effective medicines management';
- 'ensure safe and effective practice through comprehensive knowledge of medicines, their actions, risks and benefits';
- 'administer medicines safely in a timely manner, including controlled drugs';
- 'work in partnership with patient/clients and carers in relation to concordance and managing their medicines';
- 'use and evaluate up-to-date information on medicines management and work within national and local policies';
- 'through simulation and coursework, demonstrate knowledge and application of the principles required for safe and effective supply and administration via a patient group direction including an understanding of role and accountability';
- 'through simulation and course work demonstrate how to supply and administer via a patient group direction'.

Actors

Also known as 'standardized patients', actors are trained to perform in a particular role and are paid by the university. They will be very realistic and will be 'in role' throughout the examination period. They are trained to portray a patient and are used during exams that are assessing non-invasive physical examinations, interviewing skills, patient education and/or communication skills. They are normally used in OSCEs when the patient needs to play a complex role – for example, in a non-medical prescribing OSCE, assessment of a mental health condition or breaking bad news. Therefore, you will probably not often see this type of patient used in pre-registration OSCEs as they are very costly.

Practice staff

Professional practice staff may be used and they will play a similar role to standardized patients. They will not ask you any more detailed questions than any other model, even though their knowledge base will be greater. So do not be intimidated if you have a practice staff member to use as a model.

> ### Example 3: a practice staff member as a 'patient'
>
> Daniel is an experienced mentor, however, he has just moved to a new NHS trust and the students he is now mentoring attend a different HEI. He is due to mentor a third-year learning disability student nurse in the next semester and during his mentor update the facilitator informed him that the student will be required to undertake a medicines management OSCE during his placement.
>
> Daniel wanted to find out what this involved so he could support the student with their learning. The facilitator suggested to Daniel that the best way would be to become involved in the OSCE as a patient so he could gain some understanding of what the OSCE required and the level of knowledge and skills his student would be expected to demonstrate.
>
> Daniel found the experience interesting and it provided him with some very valuable CPD. He was fully aware of what would be expected from his student and consequently he felt in a better position to support them when they arrived in his practice area.
>
> When the student arrived, Daniel suggested that during the administration of medicines they would use the university checklist as an aid to ensure that the student undertook the correct practice. This meant that his student was continually being assessed using the same criteria and they could work on any gaps in knowledge and skills together.

Manikins

Lifelike manikins, anatomical models and clinical simulators may be used during the OSCE to assess problem-solving, critical thinking skills and psychomotor skills.

There are a range of manikins available:

- *Task trainer:* part of a manikin designed for a specific psychomotor skill, such as a 'resuscitation Annie', used to demonstrate your cardio-pulmonary resuscitation (CPR) skills, or a simulated arm to demonstrate venepuncture or cannulation (see Photograph 3).
- *Basic manikin:* a full body simulator without human qualities such as breathing sounds or pulses, but with the ability to have a urinary catheter NG tube, etc. inserted (see Photograph 4).

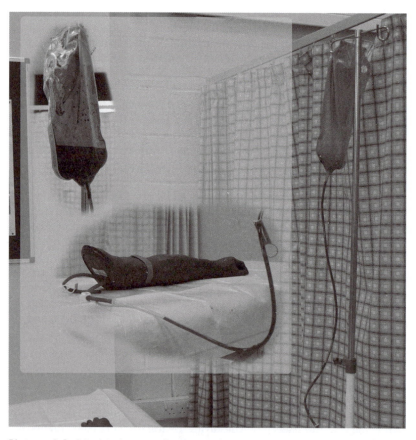

Photograph 3 A task trainer arm for cannulation or venepuncture

- *Patient simulator:* a full body simulator that can be programmed to respond to affective and psychomotor changes and has installed human qualities (e.g. breathing and cardiac sounds) (see Photographs 5 and 6).

Task trainers and manikins are normally used when the OSCE requires you to perform an invasive procedure which would not be appropriate to perform on a 'live volunteer' as it would cause them unnecessary harm and hence would be unethical. Task trainers and manikins will be chosen to meet the requirements of the OSCE. There is now a large range of these available and it will depend upon your HEI's resources as to what type you will come across. Each task trainer/manikin will have its strengths and limitations and it is therefore essential that you practise with the task trainer/manikin that you will be using during your exam. Therefore, as with all equipment, ensure you find out if you will be required to use a task trainer or manikin during your OSCE, and if so which type.

> If you are required to perform any aspect of your OSCE using a manikin or task trainer, ascertain which one you will be using and ensure you are familiar with it and have practised performing the skills using it.

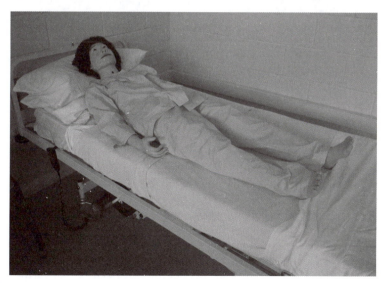

Photograph 4 A basic manikin

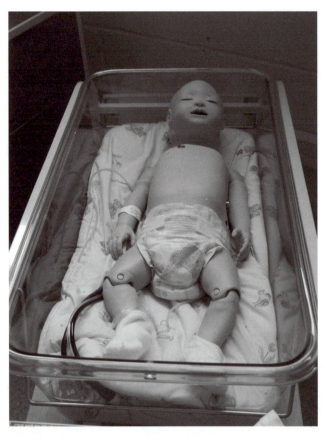

Photograph 5   SimBaby – medium-fidelity simulator

The 'resuscitation Annie' and simulated arm may be used when the OSCE is assessing a psychomotor skill only. Therefore, you are being assessed *only* on your psychomotor skills and not your communication and interpersonal skills. When using a basic full body manikin the examiner may be looking for evidence of *behaviour* as well as *performance* on the manikin. A scenario may have been designed for you to work through which will involve the manikin and possibly supplementary equipment.

When a medium-fidelity simulator such as 'SimMan', 'SimBaby' or high-fidelity 'MetiMan' is used, this will entail you working through a scenario and interpreting what responses the manikin makes. The manikin will record what actions you take

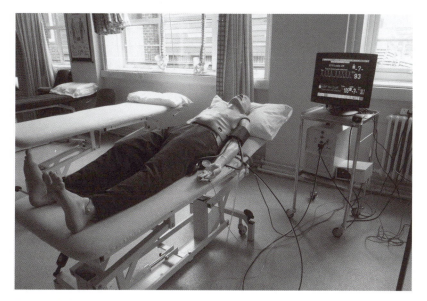

Photograph 6 A medium-fidelity manikin

for marking after the OSCE. The manikin will have been pre-programmed to give you a set of results/responses to interpret. Once again, you will be assessed on your attitude and behaviour as well as performance of the required psychomotor skills.

Computer/web-based OSCEs

Web-based OSCEs are becoming increasingly common and as such you need to know what will be required. They can include multimedia and interactive information accessed from around the world, or a stand-alone program. Common computer-based examinations are multiple choice questions or drug calculation examinations where software packages such as 'Authentic World' can be utilized. Diagram 4.1 illustrates how a computer question may be laid out.

Types of OSCE

This section will discuss what is to be expected from the various types of OSCE and the differences between them.

Regular prescription medicines			DATE
MEDICINE (Approved name) Aspirin	Start date 14/04/10		15.04.10
DOSE 75MG	ROUTE ORAL	SPECIAL INSTRUCTIONS -	
DOCTORS SIGNATURE	PHARMACY SUPPLY		08.00
Dr Smith	A Person		

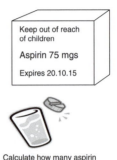

Keep out of reach of children

Aspirin 75 mgs

Expires 20.10.15

Calculate how many aspirin tablets you are required to administer

Diagram 4.1 Illustration of a calculation required in a medicines management software package

Observed OSCE

This is currently the most common type of OSCE. It may involve stations or areas where you are examined on a one-to-one basis with an independent examiner and live models or manikins as patients. The whole process is standardized so that you can be assessed objectively and complex skills and associated knowledge can be assessed without endangering any patient's health or well-being.

You may be asked to demonstrate a wide range of skills and the level of competence and knowledge you will be expected to show depends on which stage you are at in your course. For example, during the first year of a pre-registration course you may be asked to carry out a simple skill such as temperature reading and recording and explain to the examiner your findings.

In your second year you may have to teach this skill to a first-year nursing student, explaining the procedure but at the same time providing rationale and knowledge related to the skill. Photograph 2 on page 71 shows a student being observed carrying out a temperature reading. You will see that the examiner is standing in close proximity to the student so that she can carry out a comprehensive assessment of her performance. The examiner is also holding a clipboard which will have the checklist for her to make comments and assessments during the OSCE.

We found, in research of student nurses' experiences of OSCEs, that both the fact that the student was being watched so closely and the examiner was taking notes increased the student's anxieties and nerves. However, the students fully understood why it was necessary and commented that if you are fully prepared for your OSCE in relation to knowledge, skills, attitude and what to expect, these nerves can can be overcome (Merriman 2007).

> Although you are being watched closely, being well prepared helps you overcome any nerves this may cause.

Computer-assisted OSCE

This method can be formatted in several ways, for example, one of the OSCE stations could be a computer-generated multiple-choice questionnaire testing your level of knowledge of the anatomy and physiology related to the skills you have just performed. It could also be medicine calculation software, or practice area management scenarios. These types of station may well be undertaken under exam conditions in a computer room rather than a skills laboratory. You will be shown how to log onto the relevant program and then be asked to complete the task.

An alternative computer-assisted OSCE station might use an advanced manikin such as 'SimMan', described earlier, or the 'resuscitation Annie skills trainer', as they require computer software for them to work. At the same time they record your actions and this record will be used to support your assessment. Photograph 7 shows a resuscitation Annie skills trainer used to assess your CPR skills. Such a trainer could also be used in a basic life support OSCE. The examiner would assess your attitude and skills, and whether you approach the situation in a systematic way. The computer software gives the examiner feedback on the accuracy of your CPR skills – for example, if your compressions are the correct rate and depth.

Video-recording

Video-recording may be used in any OSCE situation to help the examiners in determining the level of your performance. The fact that video-recording is taking place during your OSCE can often increase your nerves; however, it is an excellent learning resource for you. Chapter 7 offers advice on how to make the best use of video footage.

Recording can take place with or without the examiners present. If the examiner is not present, the video will be reviewed at a later stage by an experienced examiner who will then make a judgement as to the level of your performance using the predetermined marking criteria. The video can also be used for quality assurance – for example, internal and external moderation – and for

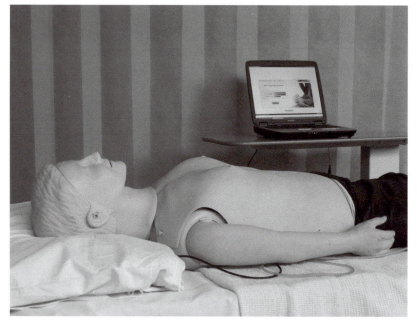

Photograph 7 'Resus Annie' skills trainer for basic life support assessment

external examiner purposes, which will be explained in more detail later in this chapter.

There is a range of different video equipment available and the type that you see will depend on your university. It may be that there is video equipment already installed in the rooms in various places, such as above the bed spaces (see Photograph 8). This type of equipment is less intrusive for you as a student as it is operated remotely and therefore you do not have someone operating the camera in the examination room. It is often small and away from the eye-line and most students say that they forget it is there.

The alternative is a traditional video camera on a tripod which requires someone to operate it. This type of equipment can be quite intrusive for you as a student so it is suggested that you gain experience of this prior to your OSCE.

Find out if your OSCE will be video-recorded and if so whether an examiner will be there as well.

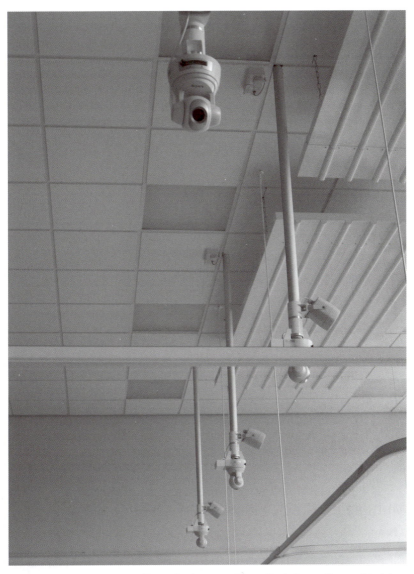

Photograph 8 Video system: Example shows scotia medical observation and training system (SMOTS)

Oral/viva

An oral examination or 'viva' may be the sole examination technique or it may be used to further test your knowledge both during and after the OSCE. The examiner will ask you pre-set questions to test your knowledge and attitude related to one or more of the stations you have just rotated around. The examiner has a list of areas they expect to cover and prepared answers which will be used to assess your responses. If you have a viva/oral as one of your stations it is advisable to ascertain what type of questions you will be asked and the level of answers you are expected to provide.

Examiner questions

Any or all of the following questions may be asked, in order to provide the student with an opportunity to further demonstrate their knowledge or attitude, during or following a medicines mangement OSCE.

- What is meant by the term 'informed consent' and how can this be achieved?
- What information do you need to obtain from the British National Formulary (BNF) and the patient before administering any medicines?
- What is meant by the term 'concordance' and how can this be achieved?
- Why is it important to confirm and document if a patient has any allergies?
- What checks would you make in order to confirm the correct identification of a patient? Why would you use these approaches?
- What are the professional and legal responsibilities of the nurse in relation to clinical records?

Multiple choice questions/short answer papers

As with a viva/oral exam a multiple choice or short answer paper may be also be the sole examination technique or may be used to further test your knowledge during or after the OSCE. Multiple choice questions and short answer papers are *objective tests* as the answers are predetermined. This means they are quick to mark and in some cases computer software can mark them. These assessment strategies are often used as they can measure a range of levels of function, such as knowledge in relation to anatomy and physiology, principles of evidence-based practice, and decision-making. Chapter 6 provides an example of a multiple choice paper that is used as a station during a basic life support OSCE. If your OSCE involves multiple choice questions or a short answer paper, most universities will have some sample papers for you to access in order to practise. Such practice is essential as it will help you with your preparation by making you aware of the level of knowledge required, thus enabling you to bring your own knowledge up to that standard (or above!).

> If you are required to sit a multiple choice or short answer paper as part of your OSCE, ensure you get hold of and complete some practice papers prior to the exam.

The examiners' role and quality assurance

Quality assurance is an area that you may not think of initially, but it is of great importance in terms of fairness of approach and the mechanisms by which you can assess the quality of your experience.

All examiners will be fully prepared for the OSCE station they are to examine prior to you undertaking the process. They will all have a set format which includes predetermined marking criteria to work to, and as such any bias and unusual questions will be minimized. The examiners may be known to you and may be academic or professional practice staff, but they may also be trained patients.

The purpose of the examiner is to assess you against the predetermined marking criteria to ascertain if you have met the required standard. The predetermined checklist is discussed in detail in Chapters 3 and 6. This structured marking criteria will enable consistency among examiners; however, the following strategies will also be in place to ensure reliability and aid quality assurance.

- All examiners will have received a copy of the predetermined marking criteria well in advance and have had an opportunity to ask questions.
- All examiners will have been briefed on the format of the OSCE they are examining so that internal reliability can been demonstrated. This is especially important during OSCEs when two or more circuits of the same stations are required.
- Examiners who are assessing the same station in different circuits are required to liaise with each other to ensure consistency in their approach. This ensures

that examiners are not influenced by their own values and beliefs, thereby promoting internal moderation and inter-observer reliability.

- Instructions that examiners give to you as students for the station they are examining will have been agreed beforehand and will often be read from script to ensure consistency.
- It is also good practice to have a moderator who moves around the examination room and observes the examiners. This ensures that all examiners are performing their role correctly.

Example 4: examiners' role in undertaking OSCEs

Jill, Darren, Ben, Stacey and David are all tutors undertaking OSCE assessments today. The first four are all examining the same station but on different circuits, and David is acting as a roving moderator for the day. This role requires David to make sure he checks that all four staff are asking the same questions of students and that they are marking to the same standard.

David notices that Ben has marked a student down on the knowledge they showed when being asked about a condition. He asks Ben what he expected the student to know and finds that Ben was requiring too much detail. They agree that what the student said was in fact sufficient and the student was then passed.

The examiners will not be able to engage in conversation with you other than to give you instructions and, if appropriate for that OSCE station, ask you the predetermined questions. They will not be able to help you beyond reasonable support, as all examiners must behave in the same way. The examiner is not trying to be intimidating, but they have to act professionally during the OSCE and ensure that they treat each student equally. They do not want to give you any false feedback, so will not give non-verbal gestures as one would normally do during conversations. For example, if they were to ask you to clarify something or ask you a question, they will just say 'thank you' and not give you any indication that may suggest you have given a correct, or incorrect, answer.

As the examiner assesses your performance against the predetermined marking criteria they will be making notes and/or ticking/crossing the relevant boxes on the assessment sheet. Do not be alarmed by this; do not automatically think that if you see them writing something you have done something wrong!

> The examiner is not trying to be intimidating: they have to act professionally during the OSCE and ensure that they treat each student equally.

Recording OSCEs

As discussed earlier in this chapter, many settings have a video system in place recording the OSCE process. If this is the case, you will be alerted to it beforehand. The system is very useful for examiners to show to external examiners. External examiners are staff from another HEI and are employed to monitor quality processes and ensure parity and fairness. The video may also be used by the examiner to check back on your performance if they are seeking advice from another examiner regarding your actions or something you said, or if they want to check whether or not you did something. The video may also be accessible to you to show how you performed, as illustrated in Photograph 9. You will find this particularly useful if you have not performed as well as you had hoped and wish to see in more detail where you could have improved your performance. Chapter 7 will discuss in greater detail how you can use video footage to support your development.

Example 5: video feedback

Jerrome had undertaken an OSCE in hand-washing. Madhur, the OSCE examiner, assessed Jerrome and was unsure whether he had undertaken all the parts of the hand-washing correctly. Once Jerrome and the other students had left the room Madhur watched the video recording of the OSCE to be completely sure of Jerrome's technique.

In the video she was able to see that Jerrome did not wash his thumbs correctly and so was quite sure that he had not met the required standard for a pass. Following the release of the results Madhur was able to go through the video with Jerrome and show him in detail where he had not met the standard required for safe practice.

It is well documented that watching our self-performance is a valuable aid in reflection, and reflection is a critical component following an OSCE. It is especially important if you fail, as it allows you to learn from your mistakes, thereby developing your practice.

When Jerrome undertook the OSCE on the next occasion, he passed.

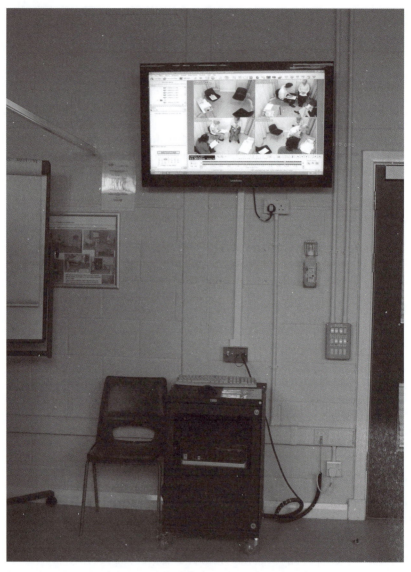

Photograph 9 An example of a video image

Your role-behaviour and performance

Your role in an OSCE is to primarily undertake safe practice, and of course to be as successful as possible! Your behaviour in the exam is also encompassed in the ESCs 'provide care that is delivered in a warm, sensitive and compassionate way', and 'listen, and provide information that is clear, accurate and meaningful at a level at which the patient/client can understand'. Your behaviour is also determined by these standards of proficiency: 'be open and honest, act with integrity and uphold the reputation of your profession'.

Health and safety is also paramount and it is essential that you listen to the advice you are given prior to commencing the OSCE. In particular, if you are using any electrical equipment you must ensure you are able to use it safely and, if unsure, that you seek assistance. If at any time during the OSCE you are putting yourself or anyone else at risk, the examiner will stop the exam immediately, which will normally result in you failing that particular OSCE station.

Professional skills

As indicated earlier, it is of utmost importance that you maintain confidentiality once you leave the examination setting. The importance of confidentiality in particular relates to the ESC 'protect and treat as confidential all information relating to themselves and their care'.

You may have heard or observed your peers when they were being examined but you are not allowed to disclose what you saw or heard. Any breach in this could affect the models used but also adversely affect the students taking part. *You should only disclose any details to the examiners present.*

Even if your OSCE is assessing a particular skill such as blood pressure measurement, and a live model is being utilized, most checklists will have an outcome related to professional behaviour and communication. This is normally an essential part of the criteria. Therefore, if you fail to meet the required standard in this section, you will fail the OSCE even if you perform the blood pressure correctly.

You can see from the example below how these aspects may be assessed. Table 4.1 illustrates the performance expected of the student by the examiner, such as asking what the patient would like to be called. In this example the achievement of a pass grade requires all components in bold to be demonstrated as a minimum. There is also a *commentary in italics* to illustrate in more detail what the examiner will be looking for in these areas.

Table 4.1 Example of how professional and communication skills can be assessed as part of an OSCE even when a psychomotor skill is the principal assessment

Activity	Performance expected	Explanation of performance expected
Professional behaviour	**Behaves in a professional manner, respecting others and adopting non-discriminatory behaviour**	*This is a key component of professional behaviour and is a core area in the standards of proficiency and ESCs. You will be expected to treat the patient with respect and ensure that personal judgements, prejudices, values, attitudes and beliefs do not compromise the care you give during the OSCE.*
	Adheres to the university professional dress code	*Each university will have worked with local trusts to write a suitable dress code for students. This has important health and safety considerations and so is not written casually. It is important when you undertake the OSCE that you wear the correct uniform so that you can illustrate that you understand the importance of the policy and implica-tions for health and safety for you and your clients.*
	Demonstrates understanding of professionalism through their practice	*This is evidence of your ability to act as a professional through your communication skills, both verbal and non-verbal. It will be visible also through the sensitive way you treat your patient.*
Communication skills	Introduces themselves to patient, giving name and status	*These two areas ensure that you take a person-centred approach.*
	Asks what patient would like to be called	
	Clarity of voice	*These sections are where the examiner is looking for clear interactions with the patient. Communication which is clear and easily heard is what the examiner is looking for – so don't mumble!!*

	Good eye contact, appropriate use of touch	*Make sure you sound authoritative and knowledgeable even if you are nervous!*
	Uses open-ended questions	
	Offers clear answers to any questions the patient may ask	
	Seeks patient's permission/consent to carry out observations	*This area is classed as essential as it demonstrates an ability to treat the patient as an individual who has rights to be treated only if they wish to be.*
	Checks patient identity: verbally, and/or with ID bracelet	*This section is paramount to ensure you are undertaking practice on the patient you are expecting to and that observations recorded or medication given is administered to the right person.*
	Checks patient's understanding of procedures	*In this section the examiner is looking for you to check that the patient has understood what you have told them and this will be assisted if you have not used jargon and terminology that the patient may not have come across.*
	Clear explanation given throughout, no jargon used	

Unfairness or discrimination

If you feel you have not been treated fairly you may be able to access a video-recording of the exam and review how you performed. If there is no recording you will need to seek the view of the examination lead to ascertain how you can lodge your concerns about unfair behaviour. You need to refer to your university policy concerning how to lodge an appeal or complaint.

Chapter summary

1 You should have an idea of the room and station layout before you start the OSCE.

2 You should be aware of and familiar with any equipment or documentation you will be required to use.

3 You should understand the set guidelines and protocols for your OSCE.

4 You need to behave in a professional manner at all times during your OSCE.

5 Your models may be members of the general public, staff, manikins or task trainers.

6 All patient models will be working to the same ground rules to ensure parity.

7 The examination process is governed by strict quality assurance mechanisms to ensure objectivity.

8 You may be videoed during the examination for quality assurance and also for feedback for you to learn from.

9 Try not to use jargon that the patient may not understand.

10 If you feel you have not been treated fairly, you may be able to access a video recording of the event and review how you performed.

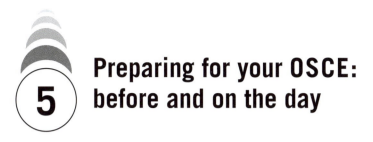

Preparing for your OSCE: before and on the day

5

Diligence is the mother of good luck.

Benjamin Franklin (1706–90)

By the end of this chapter you will:

○ Understand how to prepare for your OSCE.
○ Understand how to perform to the best of your ability.
○ Have gained insight into how stress will affect your performance.
○ Have gained insight into how to make the most use of the stress you are under to enhance your performance.
○ Have worked through the 10 steps for preparation.

This chapter will provide you with guidance on how to prepare for your OSCE and also how to perform to the best of your ability during the exam. First, it will look at how to prepare to ensure you have the relevant knowledge, skills and attitude to meet the criteria set by the examiners. Within this section suggestions will be given to help you identify when and how you learn and work most effectively. During any exam a certain amount of stress is normal and essential in order to give you the motivation to learn and perform – therefore, a discussion will take place to help you identify the differences between optimum and sub-optimum stress levels. The remainder of the chapter will help you prepare for the day of the exam – for example, in terms of dress code, coping mechanisms, travel arrangements, and so on, in order to ensure that you perform to the best of your ability on the day.

Prior preparation

Whenever you are preparing for an important event it is useful to remember to address the five 'Ps': *'prior preparation prevents poor performance'*. This mnemonic will give you every chance to be successful. Every assessment, including OSCEs, will assess several components – for example, skills, knowledge and attitude. Therefore you will have to prepare yourself for all of these areas to ensure you pass. Find out as much as you can about the format and content of your exams and how they will be assessed. It's important to know what is required from you, so there are no nasty shocks on the day.

Students undertaking OSCEs have said to us that, 'If you do not know your "stuff", then you are not going to pass the OSCE, whereas if you know your "stuff", then the OSCE will not be a problem.'

> Prior preparation prevents poor performance.

It is the desire to pass the OSCE that will give you the motivation to learn the required skills. It is a well-known fact within educational theory that assessment methods and requirements have a greater influence on how and what you as a student learn than any other single factor (Boud and Brew 1995; Gibbs and Simpson 2004). The external rewards and punishments for not passing the OSCE are probably what are motivating you to learn, as much as intrinsic factors such as authentic interest and involvement in the subject matter.

Therefore, it is the motivation of *not wanting to fail* that will drive and direct your behaviour as much as anything else. This is not to say that you are not interested in the subject matter, but *you* have not chosen to master this subject area – it has been chosen for you, either by your professional body or the HEI itself.

To be successful in your OSCE, you need to have what is called 'intrinsic motivation'. That is, you feel you want to be successful because it makes you feel good and you want to achieve a goal. There will also be an element of *extrinsic motivation*, which is a factor that is almost always present and will also help you succeed. This includes a desire to get a 'good pass' because others want you to be successful, and the fact that you want to qualify as a nurse or pass the particular course you are undertaking in order to get a good job.

Both forms of motivation are useful. Ideally, a combination of both is best – your interest in a topic along with pressure from outside sources, such as the HEI or peers to be successful, are strong motivating factors.

> Your motivation to learn may be just to pass the OSCE, but try to be both intrinsically and extrinsically motivated.

Once you have worked out what you are required to know and do to ensure you meet the set criteria to pass, you can map out your time and effort with greater efficiency. Therefore it is essential that you study the assessment criteria and checklist to ensure you are aware of what level of performance and knowledge the examiners want you to demonstrate in your OSCE. In order to ensure that you are aware of this, you need to use the resources discussed in Chapters 2, 3 and 4, such as accessing practical sessions, formative assessment, the marking criteria and checklists.

> Make good use of all the help available to assist you in preparing well.

Stress and your ability to manage it

Once you have highlighted what you know and what you don't know, be under no illusion that stress will kick in to ensure that your body is ready to perform. You need to ensure that you have the optimum level of stress *for you*. You will have different stress levels to your peers. You will also get stressed at different times depending on your personality, your motivation and drive to do well, and among other things your personal circumstances. So don't compare yourself with others but be aware of your own stress and more importantly of how *you* find it best to manage this.

How stress is manifested in the body

Some people can lead busy, tightly-scheduled lives without appearing to suffer from excessive stress, whereas others who have routine, uncomplicated lives can feel a great deal of stress. Excessive stress increases the rate at which your body produces cortisol. Cortisol is a corticosteroid hormone produced by the adrenal gland. The main role of cortisol is to activate the immune system. It is involved also with the metabolism of glucose, and can cause elevation of the blood sugar level. Excess cortisol is known to increase catabolism (protein breakdown in muscles): the cortisol leads to muscle breakdown through promoting a release of muscle amino acids for transport to the liver, where the amino acids are converted into glucose (Waugh and Grant 2006). Cortisol is part of the body's response to stress. However, it is important that the body can return to normal following stressful events. It is unfortunate that, in our current highly-stressed lives, the body's stress response is activated so frequently that the body's functions don't always have a chance to return to normal. This can result in a state of *chronic stress* (Scott 2008). Levels of cortisol in the bloodstream that are higher and prolonged (similar to those linked with chronic stress) have been shown to have adverse effects, such as impaired cognitive performance and blood sugar imbalances such as hyperglycaemia. Excessive levels of cortisol in your body can cause you to feel confused and can reduce your ability to distinguish between what is important and what is not. For example, you may focus on the set of skills you are required to demonstrate in your exam and forget other important areas such as communication skills. Your brain can lose some of its ability to sort out what is new information, to retrieve old information and to perform certain skills that you already have. Your thinking becomes more automatic and your brain struggles to link new knowledge with the skills you are trying to learn. Hence it is hard to learn anything new as the cortisol is impeding the deployment of your thinking skills.

> The body needs to return to normal following stress to prevent chronic stress and its side-effects.

Consequently, excessive stress impairs your ability to learn, your ability to think, and your memory and problem-solving skills, all of which are needed to help you prepare for and perform adequately during your OSCE. However, at the same time you will need a certain amount of stress to aid your drive and motivation to learn; therefore, you need to find your optimal stress level to ensure the efficiency of your learning and effectiveness of your performance.

Diagram 5.1 demonstrates the relationship between levels of stress and efficiency. You can see that we all need some level of stress to increase our efficiency, however, too much stress, incorrectly managed, will cause reduced efficiency levels and eventually burnout.

How stress can be displayed

Stress can be displayed by both physical and psychological symptoms. In order for you to recognize and try and reduce these you need to be aware of them (see Table 5.1). You will not necessarily display them all, however, if you do recognize any, you need to ascertain a way of reducing the symptoms. Remember it is not always possible to remove the cause of the stress; it is how you deal with it that matters. Before you act to reduce stress, you need to distinguish between helpful levels of stress and excessive levels of stress.

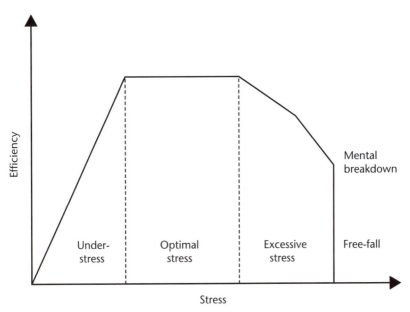

Diagram 5.1 The relationship between under-stress, optimal stress, excessive stress and efficiency

Stress levels need to be fine-tuned, not eliminated (as highlighted in Diagram 5.1) in order to ensure efficiency. As well as producing cortisol in the body, stress also helpfully releases the hormones of adrenaline and noradrenaline. These have the effect of improving perception, motivation and performance, all of which are needed to help you prepare for and perform adequately in your exam. So it's not all bad news from the point of view of the body's response!

Example 1: managing stress

Jim had undertaken a formative OSCE in December and had found he was extremely stressed during it. He was unable to talk coherently and fumbled when he tried to take his patient's pulse. This worried Jim as he did not want to fail his summative attempt.

Jim decided to try to manage his stress more actively so that he could get the most out of being stressed rather than let it overcome him. He had read that yoga was a good way to relax so he enrolled for a number of classes. The yoga taught him several mechanisms which he could use to relieve his stress when it started to build up. He felt calmer and more in control.

When Jim undertook his summative OSCE he felt more in control and was able to undertake all the parts of the exam at a pass level.

It is uncomfortable to realize that there are some situations that can push stress beyond helpful levels, and these include embarrassment, perceived loss of status or a belief that a task is impossible. Unhelpful levels of stress are more likely when you think there is not enough time to complete a task to the standard required. For example, if you do not start to prepare for your exam with enough time to meet the requirements, you may display unhelpful levels of stress during the period leading up to the OSCE and during the OSCE.

To keep cortisol levels healthy and under control you should activate the body's relaxation response when undue stress occurs. As preparation for the OSCE and the exam itself will require you to make a number of decisions, the extra time needed to do the preparation could be gained by taking the decision more quickly. However, because thinking becomes slower under excessive levels of stress, it takes longer to make the decisions in the first place and this, as you can imagine, creates a vicious circle. If you try to make up for the shortage of time and the slower thinking speed by giving less thought to the decisions, you increase the number of thoughtless decisions. This raises anxiety about the risk of mistakes and further raises the level of stress experienced. Table 5.1 shows both the physical symptoms and the psychological symptoms of stress. You can see there are multiple effects on both the body and the mind, and so any mechanism to manage this will help you to attempt your OSCE more successfully.

Even when you have your anxiety at an optimum level, raised your expectations and removed some of the sources of excessive stress, it will still require a deliberate amount of effort on your part to improve your ability to concentrate in order to prepare for your exam. You need to think about when you concentrate best. Are you a morning, afternoon or night person? Whatever you are, you cannot easily change your daily pattern of concentration, and therefore you need to work around it and make the most of your daily cycle. This means scheduling study time around the peak times when you know you function most effectively. At this point it may be useful to go back to Chapter 3 and remind yourself of your own learning style analysis.

Table 5.1 The physical and psychological effects of stress

Physical	Psychological
General aches and pains, including backache	Feeling inadequate
Excessive sweating, constipation and diarrhoea	Difficulty in concentrating
Frequent indigestion or heartburn	Feeling anxious, apprehensive or irritable
Insomnia and constant tiredness	Increasing difficulty in making important decisions
Lack of appetite or overeating	Poor retrieval of memory
Sexual impotence	
Migraine attacks	
Asthma attacks	

How environmental factors will affect you

Environmental factors are also important. Think about your levels of tolerance to distraction and decide whether you like background noise when you study or whether you need complete silence; can you manage with peers or children around, or do you need to be alone? Sometimes, finding a quiet area when you are living in student accommodation or in a busy household is difficult, so remember that sudden intermittent noises are more distracting to your brain than consistent high background noise. It is the level of intermittent noise relative to the background noise level that is the key here. Therefore, you may *think* that you study best without music playing, but playing music that mutes sudden intermittent noises may be beneficial to your concentration. Background music has been found to reduce mental fatigue and improve concentration, however, this is only true if it is well matched to the thinking task in hand and to your preference as an individual.

Example 2: managing revision time effectively

Carl is a 35-year-old father of three children aged 5, 8 and 10 and has to revise for his OSCE. He is finding the children's noise very distracting and they are getting fed up with him telling them to be quiet.

He realizes that asking the children to be silent is not an option, and so makes a plan for some quieter, but not silent, time. Instead of revising in the room where the children are playing, he moves his work into the bedroom and puts on some background music. He negotiates with them that if they play quietly for one hour at a time he will play with them later. The background noise is reduced by the music and by having an hour at a time of concentrated work Carl can revise more efficiently. He then does not feel guilty about not paying the children much attention as he has agreed a concentrated play time with them afterwards.

Communal background music may impair the thinking ability of some people who need absolute quiet. Hence, ideally, 'music while you work' should be through individual headsets. Think about what type of music you find most relaxing so that you can concentrate on your work and not listen to the music. One of the authors listened to music by Mozart when studying and now whenever that music is played she can remember the work she was revising!

Light affects your mood and therefore your mental energy, mental alertness and speed of thinking. Light tells your pineal gland to stop producing melatonin. This is a good thing because melatonin literally sends your brain to sleep. Therefore, if you are using resources such as books or computers to increase your knowledge base, or just practising clinical skills, do you dim your lights or use shuttle lighting? Think again, as for brainwork you need bright light, preferably natural light. If your natural light needs to be supplemented with artificial lighting, try and use full spectrum 'blue' tubes. This may help you to concentrate more efficiently and for a longer period of time.

Nutrition and feeding your brain

Nutrition, hydration and change of environment are also important when studying. Having a well-balanced diet is important as dehydration and lack of food make it difficult for the brain to work and can cause poor concentration and increase stress. Studying is tiring, even exhausting, as the primary source of energy in the human brain, glucose, can be rapidly used up during mental activity.

Mental concentration drains glucose from a key part of the brain associated with memory and learning, highlighting how crucial optimum blood sugar is for proper brain function. Glucose is the form of sugar that travels in your bloodstream to fuel the brain and is the only fuel normally used by brain cells. Because neurons cannot store glucose, they depend on the bloodstream to deliver a constant supply of this precious fuel. This blood sugar is obtained from carbohydrates: the starches and sugars you eat in the form of grains and legumes, fruits and vegetables.

It is therefore essential that you provide your brain with a constant supply of glucose by eating foods with a low glycaemic index number, which *gradually* release glucose into your bloodstream. This gradual release helps minimize blood sugar swings and optimizes brainpower and mental focus. These foods include oats, brown pasta and rice instead of white, beans, vegetables, white fish, chicken and turkey.

A sugary snack or soft drink that quickly raises your blood sugar level gives you a boost (and any caffeine adds to the lift), but it's short-lived. When you eat something with high sugar content your pancreas starts to secrete insulin. Insulin triggers cells throughout your body to pull the excess glucose out of your bloodstream and store it for later use. Soon, the glucose available to your brain has dropped. Hence too much sugar or refined carbohydrates at one time can actually deprive your brain of glucose, depleting its energy supply and compromising your brain's power to concentrate, remember and learn. So however tempting it may be to reach for the chocolate, it is better to have an oat bar or apple instead.

Example 3: managing diet more effectively

Hannah liked to eat biscuits and sweets when revising as she felt she needed a boost when working. She found that she was putting on weight and also experiencing headaches and tiredness more often than normal. She wondered if this was related to her diet and so decided to try eating low glycaemic index food for a week to see if it made a difference.

Hannah made sure she:

- had low glycaemic index cereal for breakfast like porridge;
- substituted apples and grapes instead of chocolate for a snack;
- had baked beans on brown toast for lunch;
- had fish or chicken for supper.

Although Hannah missed her sweet food, she did feel more alert and less tired. She allowed herself her favourite chocolate bar once she had taken her OSCE.

Hydration: why you need to keep drinking!

A simple tip to prevent dehydration is to fill a litre water bottle at the beginning of the day, keep it with you and ensure you have drunk it before you go to bed in the evening. This will need to be supplemented with other liquids, but try and reduce the amount of tea, coffee or caffeine-related drinks you consume as caffeine causes the body to lose water (diuresis), and hence can increase the risk of dehydration. An important factor to remember is that thirst is a sign of dehydration, so try to drink *before* you are thirsty.

The importance of exercise

You may think you don't have any time for exercise, but there is no doubt that it's a really good way to unwind and feel fresher for your studies. It may be hard to find time to exercise, particularly during exams when all you seem to do is sit at your desk and work all day (and into the night). However, not only is exercise good for your overall health and fitness, it also boosts your mental well-being. Hence it will reduce stress and improve concentration. Exercise will have the added effect of helping to keep you calm during exams. You'll feel more energized and refreshed and this in turn will help you to perform more effectively in your studies. You don't need to make a special trip to a sports centre to reach your weekly quota of exercise – there are easy ways to introduce some exercise into your daily routine. So try to plan your day and fit some exercise around your study time.

Here are some suggestions.

- Walk to your lectures instead of getting the bus.
- Take the stairs rather than the lift.
- If you have a bike, ride it to classes or go for a bike ride with friends.
- Rent or buy an exercise DVD. Share the cost – and fun – with your housemates.
- If you're going out in the evening, dance. It's a great way to meet new friends as well as keep in shape.
- Go for a jog with friends before going to college, or between classes.
- At lunchtime or weekends, kick a football around with your friends in the park, or have a game of volleyball.
- Clean your flat or house! Housework is a great way to keep fit and should involve stretching, etc.

- Try taking small, regular breaks to refresh yourself and clear your mind. Try a walk to the library or around campus.
- You could also try to exercise first thing in the morning. You may find it wakes you up and gives you energy for the day.
- Try swimming or doing some stretching exercises.

Ten simple steps to success

So now you have an understanding of how to look after yourself to ensure optimum levels of well-being while you are preparing for your OSCE. This section looks at how you can prepare by following 10 simple steps.

1 Get organized

An important key for success in OSCEs is organization. Good time management skills will help you to become more organized and waste less time preparing to study. Here is a range of tools you can use for better time management.

- *Getting started:* the first thing is to get started on your task. It is a good idea not to procrastinate too long, otherwise you may end up failing to start work or enjoy planned leisure time. So be decisive and get down to it!
- *Have a good routine:* routine can either be a burden or a release. Make it a release for you by setting a daily time for work and revision and aim to stick to this. Often people will skip sessions if they are not properly scheduled in, so devise a timetable for work *and* leisure. The key to this is making sure that at the times you have set aside for work, you actually do some! Set yourself targets so you know what you are going to study – for example, is today going to be set aside for practising a clinical skill? Or do you plan to revise the anatomy or underpinning knowledge required to practise this skill safely?
- *Try not to say yes to commitments you can't keep:* don't feel pressurized into taking time out from work or revision just to please someone else. You need to dedicate time and not be diverted. You can be assertive and considerate when you say no, and in the long run you will be more productive. Remember this is *your* time to succeed.
- *Make time to plan your work and leisure:* items such as daily planners and university calendars will help you to know what you need to do and when you need to have it done. Try using a pie chart to organize your waking day or your week. This will allow you to visualize how you can balance studying with having a social life and family time.

Example 4: making lists to manage revision effectively

Ashanti knew that she had to revise a great deal for her medicines management OSCE but couldn't think where to start. So she decided to make a list of all the areas she wanted to work on. She then broke this down into subsections which could be undertaken in an hour. Following this she made a plan for a two-week period to make sure she could fit in enough one-hour periods of revision to cover all the areas she needed to. This meant that when she was not revising she was able to feel confident that all of her work could be accomplished in the time available and could enjoy her downtime. Ashanti had a friend's birthday in the middle of her revision and so built in time to get a present and go out for the evening as well as do her revision.

Diagram 5.2 gives you an example of how you could manage your daytime activities to make sure you build in enough time for revision. You can see that it builds in exercise time as well as time with friends, etc. This will make sure you have downtime during your revision.

2 Understand the assessment

It is important that you are aware of what you are being assessed on and what you are expected to do during the exam. You also need to know what level you will be assessed at and the format of the OSCE. It is important to be clear whether you will be expected to answer verbal questions during the exam or at

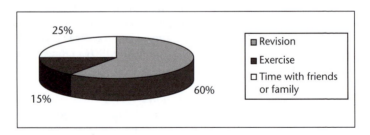

Diagram 5.2 Managing your day

the end, or to complete a written paper (Chapter 4 discusses the type of information you can expect to receive prior to your OSCE in more detail). In order to be aware of this you will need to review the module/course documentation, attend any lectures/seminars that discuss the OSCEs and review any OSCE checklist and marking criteria. You will need to clarify whether there is a simulated patient used in your exam and if so what type (see Chapter 4).

3 Start studying early

It is very important that you start preparing for your OSCEs well in advance. Even if you are a 'last-minute person', this is not the time to use such a tactic! It has been found that students who cram information at the last minute don't retain the information as well and also get tired and overloaded far more easily. So break the habit of a lifetime and make a plan which helps you to study early and often.

4 Review lecture notes

Be sure that you review your lecture notes and other information you have been given to develop the skills, knowledge and attitude to meet the criteria set for your OSCE. You should start reviewing your notes on a daily basis. This will ensure that you gradually learn, relearn and then consolidate the information over time and don't have to cram.

5 Review relevant texts

Your course textbooks and virtual learning resources are wonderful sources for finding illustrations and diagrams that will help you visualize the concepts you are learning. Be sure to reread and review the appropriate chapters and information in your textbooks and virtual learning sites. You will want to make sure that you understand all the key concepts and topics.

6 Get answers to your questions

If you are having difficulty understanding your OSCE or have unanswered questions, discuss them with your tutor. Sometimes you may think you fully understand what you need to know but on reflection, prior to the OSCE, you may be unsure. It is strongly advised that you seek help and clarification so that you are as prepared as possible. You don't want to go into an OSCE with gaps in your knowledge and revising early and clarifying the areas you are unsure of will give you plenty of time to understand the skills and knowledge you are required to master.

7 Quiz yourself

To help prepare yourself for the OSCE and find out how much you know, give yourself a quiz. You can do this by using prepared flash cards or taking a sample test prepared by your course tutors. Rehearsing answers will give you a good opportunity to see how much you know. You will have had the opportunity to practise your OSCE either in a formal formative attempt or as an informal practice. You can use the notes from these practices to make up your own quiz questions.

8 Find a 'study buddy'

Get together with a friend or classmate and have a study session. Take turns assessing each other's performance, with one of you acting as the examiner and use the OSCE checklist to mark the other student's performance. Ask them questions to assess their knowledge. By giving constructive feedback you will learn by being both the student and examiner. Why not video each other and then analyse your performances? This way, common mistakes can be ironed out and worked upon before the OSCE. Ensure, however, that any videos are not shared with anyone if all parties do not agree to this. It is strongly advised *not* to put any videos you make on any social networking sites as this may lead to questions about professional behaviour.

Example 5: using a 'study buddy'

Kayla and Naomi lived in student accommodation together and were undertaking OSCEs at the same time. They decided that they would work together to test each other's knowledge and skill. They took it in turns to be the student and the patient and they gave each other feedback as to their performance. They were undertaking hand-washing and basic observations. They weren't able to take blood pressure in their accommodation but could manage all other parts of the skill.

It felt a little weird to test each other at the start but they soon got into the practice and found it to be very valuable. It gave them an opportunity to realize what they did not know well and what they needed to learn more fully.

9 Attend any formative or OSCE preparation sessions

If you are invited to a formative OSCE, ensure you attend as this will give you valuable feedback, as discussed in Chapter 2. Added to this, if your tutors hold a review session, be sure to attend. This will help to identify specific topics that will be covered, as well as fill in any gaps in knowledge. Help sessions are also an ideal place to get answers to your questions. If formative sessions record your performance, ensure you review this, as by looking at your own performance you will be able to see more clearly where you need to improve.

10 Relax

Now that you have followed the previous steps, it's time to rest and relax. You should be well prepared for your OSCE. It's a good idea to make sure you get plenty of sleep the night before your exam. Aim to relax the evening before but do not be tempted to do so using alcohol as this may impair your performance the following day.

> You are well prepared so try to think positively!

Reducing OSCE nerves

Even if you have carried out all of the above and therefore feel you have done everything possible to ensure you are successful in your OSCE, you will still feel nervous on the day of the exam. This is normal and also essential to give you the energy and drive to perform well. Nerves are a form of stress and, as discussed earlier in the chapter, a certain amount of stress is important as it will give you the motivation and determination to perform.

What you need to do is ensure that you avoid any unnecessary stress that may tip your stress levels and hence hinder your performance on the day. Being able to answer the questions in Table 5.2 will help ensure you get to the exam on time and prepared, avoiding unnecessary stress. Once you have answered all of them you will be ready to arrive at your OSCE as you have done everything you can to ensure your performance and level of knowledge are adequate.

Table 5.2 Are you prepared for your OSCE?

A	Do I know the date and time of my OSCE?
B	Do I know what time and where I need to report for my OSCE?
C	How am I planning on travelling to the OSCE?
D	How long should it take me to get to the OSCE?
	(Always allow *longer* in case of hold-ups. Many HEIs will not allow students who are late to sit their exam, which may result in you failing a module.)
E	What am I expected to wear to the OSCE?
	Am I expected to wear my clinical uniform?
	If not, what type of clothes are practical and will aid my performance?
F	What forms of identification do I need to take?
G	What equipment/resources do I need to bring to my OSCE and what will be supplied by the HEI?

The night before the exam

The night before the exam is often the most stressful. Having a good night's sleep is important in helping you perform well during your OSCE. Here are some tips to help you sleep:

- gather together what you will need to take into the exam room (pens, water, allowed texts, calculator, student card, etc.);
- stop revising 90 minutes before preparing for bed;
- relax with friends, music, book, TV, etc.;
- have a warm bath or shower;
- use a relaxation exercise;
- if your head's still buzzing with thoughts in the middle of the night, have a notebook by the side of the bed and write them down.

How to perform well in your OSCE

This section will help ensure you stay calm during the exam. Make sure you arrive at the venue a minimum of 10 minutes before the OSCE. If you rely on public transport, make sure you get an earlier bus than required, as being late due to a cancelled bus will probably not be acceptable. Alternatively, if you are driving to the exam, make sure you have enough petrol and again leave in enough time to avoid traffic jams, etc. and to allow you to find a parking space. It is better to arrive early and have time for a calming drink and to get changed into your uniform than to be rushed!

You can help to get your mind set for the exam by:

- turning off your mobile phone;
- following the invigilator's instructions as to where to put your phone and any bags you have with you;
- checking your pockets to make sure you don't take forbidden items into the exam (e.g. notes, mobile phone, etc.).

It is normal practice for OSCEs to have a period of time before the exam for you to prepare, before you go into the simulated learning environment. This is because you may not know the exact scenario or stations you will be undertaking until the day of the exam. The amount of time you will be given depends on the complexity of the OSCE. During this time, follow these simple steps:

- read the instructions on the front of the paper carefully;
- make sure you know which scenario/stations you will be examined on;
- read the scenarios slowly, then read them again – it's all too easy to misread when you are nervous;
- ensure you understand what you have been *asked* to do rather than what you were *expecting* to do;
- where there is a choice, choose the scenario/station you think you can perform best;
- try not to panic if you are given a station/scenario you were not expecting or one that you feel is not your best;
- if you are able to, during this time make notes on key aspects as this will help you focus;
- remind yourself of the timings for the length of the OSCE and how long you should spend on each section of the exam.

During the exam

Everyone gets nervous in exams. Take a deep breath before you go in and remember these basic guidelines:

1   Even though you may be nervous or worried, listen to what the examiner in charge tells you to do. If unsure, ask for clarification.

2 Get into role and remember you are a health care professional as well as a student; this may help you with your performance.

3 Remember to take your time. Often when nerves set in we rush and this is when we make mistakes. You have been allocated a certain amount of time as this is how much the examiners feel you will need. Therefore, use this time wisely, take your time, remember the examiner is observing your skills and attitude and will also be assessing your level of knowledge.

4 Ensure you carry out every step to the highest quality possible.

5 If applicable, ensure you gain consent prior to starting the scenario, and use this opportunity to explain what the procedure will involve.

6 Narrate your way through the exam as this will show the examiner you not only know what to do but you know *why* you are doing it.

7 To demonstrate your knowledge base, ensure you relate theory to practice through your narration and if applicable offer differential diagnosis and normal and abnormal pathology.

8 If you have a viva or paper exam as part of your OSCE, ensure you read or listen to the instructions carefully. Before looking at the actual questions, read the instructions – are there any compulsory questions? Marks are often lost by nervous or over-confident students who overlook instructions.

9 Read through the paper once and then reread each question. You might think a topic you've revised hasn't come up, when it is there but the wording is unusual.

10 If you are being asked questions during the OSCE or as part of a viva and you do not know the answer instantly, you can ask the examiner to repeat the question. This will give you thinking time and also the opportunity to hear the question again; you may pick up key words that you did not register the first time.

11 If your mind goes blank during the OSCE, inform the examiner that you just need to step back and take a few seconds to gather your thoughts. You are better doing this than going on with the exam and making an error.

12 If you think that something is wrong, if you feel unwell, or if something is distracting you, inform your examiner.

13 Make sure you do not communicate with, or look at, any other candidate. You can be disqualified if you break the exam rules in any way.

14 If you finish early, spend a few seconds going through what you have done – have you missed anything? You can often rectify the situation if you are within the time, however, once you have left the room, you cannot return.

It's all a matter of positive attitude. Remember, this is your chance to perform to the very best of your ability. It's worth taking up the challenge to prove what you can do – after all, it will be over in a few hours or less.

The next chapter will take you through a range of OSCE examples and tell you what is expected of you in each one.

Chapter summary

1   Remember the five Ps – 'prior preparation prevents poor performance'.

2   Plan your revision strategy and use the tools for time management.

3   Ensure your strategy gives you ample time to revise early and often.

4   Maximize your potential by ensuring you eat, drink and relax to minimize any threat to your brain.

5   Try revising with fellow students.

6   Recognize excessive stress and reduce any unnecessary stress.

7   Read all your instructions well in advance.

8   Plan your route to the OSCE so you arrive in plenty of time.

9   Make the most of the time allocated to you.

10 If your mind goes blank during the exam, step back for a few seconds to gather your thoughts.

6 Sample OSCEs: adult basic life support, medicines management and aseptic non-touch technique

Examinations are formidable even to the best prepared, for the greatest fool may ask more than the wisest man can answer.

Charles Caleb Colton (1770–1832)

By the end of this chapter you will:

○ Understand the potential components of an OSCE assessment.
○ Be aware of the minimum standard of competency you will have to demonstrate to pass a range of OSCEs.
○ Be clear about the terminology of OSCE checklists and marking criteria and how this can help your preparation.

OSCE examples

This chapter offers you additional examples of OSCEs to the one that was provided in Chapter 3. The purpose is to demonstrate how, by breaking down your OSCE stations, checklists and marking criteria, you can be well prepared and be more successful in your exam.

The chapter offers you three examples of possible OSCE stations that you may come across in your course: 'basic life support', 'medicines management' and 'principles of aseptic non-touch technique'. Checklists and marking criteria are included for you to look at when thinking about the OCSE. A brief explanation will be given to outline the broad skills and knowledge that the OSCE is assessing and how it might be organized.

When assessing OSCEs, the examiners will be looking for certain key points. The skills and knowledge being assessed will vary but the qualities of an excellent performance during an OSCE will be the same whatever the subject. Each university will have its own checklist and assessment criteria for the OSCE, and this should be shared with you before you take the exam. You should use these assessment criteria to support your preparation for your OSCE.

The OSCE station/skill will be provided along with the OSCE checklist. This will be annotated to show what the examiner is looking for in order for you to pass that particular station.

OSCE checklists

There is no standard checklist for an OSCE station as it is up to each university to produce their own. They will make sure that OSCEs are objective in their nature and that consistency between markers is transparent. What all OSCE checklists should have in common is that they should be underpinned, wherever possible, by evidence-based guidelines and/or current policy. For example, when developing the checklist for administering medication, the marking criteria were based on the NMC *Standards for Medicines Management* (NMC 2008b).

As you perform the required skill(s) during the OSCE, the examiner will evaluate your performance using the standardized checklist. Everything you do correctly is marked against the predetermined criteria. Usually the final mark encompasses not only the marks from the checklist, but also a global rating from the examiner. This is because at every OSCE station, consideration should also be given to the patient's feelings, maintenance of dignity and establishing rapport. This is in keeping with good practice guidelines such as those evident in *Essence of Care* (DoH 2007) and the NMC Code (NMC 2008a). It is difficult to assess these elements by means of marking criteria – hence the use of a global rating which enables the examiner to comment on the subjective nature of your performance.

You will find that some OSCEs are 'pass/fail' while others are given a grade/score. The reason for this may be the type of OSCE and the stage at which you are in your course.

Assessment marking criteria

Assessment marking criteria will be used by the examiner to provide you with feedback on your performance – for example, the level of your performance or knowledge base. It could just give you guidance on your level of performance in respect to good pass, borderline pass, borderline fail, or fail, or it could have greater detail in respect to each grade (see OSCE, example 2, p. 127–8).

Marking grids can be useful for you to work out how you can achieve the highest mark possible. This type of marking criteria is usually divided into the elements you will be assessed on. If you are offered a marking grid as well as a checklist, you should use it to help you increase your score.

There are some general grading principles that can be applied to OSCEs. For example, to gain an A grade or distinction, you will need to provide an exceptional performance, with all the criteria attempted competently, and supported by an excellent knowledge base. You would provide full narration throughout your performance and demonstrate an evaluative approach.

For a B+/B grade or merit, your performance would need to be logical in relation to the skill being performed. Your performance may be flawed in a few minor aspects, but not unsafe. The quality of the performance, narration and level of knowledge base at all times would be adequate and at times good or excellent.

For a C grade or pass, you may demonstrate some inaccurate/inadequate parts of the OSCE, however, you are still safe and your knowledge base is very descriptive even though certain aspects of the OSCE did not have supporting narration. Your performance may well be loosely structured with some consequent loss of coherence in places. There may be significant lapses in presentation but these would not be bad enough to say that you are not competent.

For a referral/fail grade, you would have demonstrated an insufficient level of knowledge and/or your performance of the skills would have been inadequate with inaccuracies in style and the technicalities. You may also have demonstrated unsafe practice.

Other preparation aids

Although the OSCE stations, standardized checklists and marking criteria will support you in your preparation for your exam, you will also need to use books, literature and other resources such as DVDs or videos given to you by the university. These will support your learning in respect to performing the skills.

In addition to this you need to read *around* the skills you have been asked to perform. For example, you need to know the primary causes of common clinical signs, such as what may cause someone to have a pyrexia. Related anatomy and pathology are also essential as these are vital for you to demonstrate your underpinning knowledge and decision-making.

More importantly, you cannot study for your OSCE from reading alone. You need to practise performing the skills, go over the stages, using the criteria to help guide you, until you feel you can perform each step to at least the minimum level required. The key to success is to practise and practise, either alone or with peers.

We will now illustrate two OSCEs to help you to understand what is expected of you, and one OSCE for you to read through and see if you can work out what is required.

OSCE example 1: adult basic life support

Explanation

The purpose of this OSCE is to assess knowledge and skill in relation to basic life support. As part of your mandatory training you will be required to demonstrate that you have the skills and knowledge to care for a patient who has had a cardiac arrest and therefore this is a very common OSCE for nursing students. The Resuscitation Council Guidelines (www.resus.org.uk/pages/standard.pdf) state that all health care professionals including undergraduate students should have initial training followed by yearly updates, which include an evaluation of competency in resuscitation. As this is very difficult to assess in practice, an OSCE is a very appropriate way to assess your competence in these skills. This OSCE is assessing your skills at a very basic level and takes place in a community setting. The OSCE may increase with complexity as you progress in your course – for example, you may have to demonstrate use of an automated defibrillator or work in a resuscitation team in an acute hospital setting.

The OSCE consists of two stations that present you with a clinical situation in a community setting and are designed to evaluate your skills and knowledge in basic life support.

On station one you would be assessed against predetermined marking criteria on your performance of basic life support on a manikin. In this OSCE, station one would last five minutes.

Station two consists of a short multiple choice question paper to assess your knowledge and awareness of the key interventions of basic life support. Station two would last 10 minutes.

You can see below that you will be marked against a range of criteria and these include:

- safety;
- recognition of the unresponsive patient;
- appropriately calling for help;
- your skills in airway management including using a pocket mask;
- CPR.

Failure of one mandatory criteria will result in you failing this station as it would be deemed that you are not competent.

Station two is the multiple choice paper, and here you will be asked a range of questions related to station one to assess that you have the knowledge to underpin your skill. You need to answer 40 per cent of the questions correctly in order to pass this station.

When an OSCE has more than one station it is important for you to find out if you need to pass all stations to achieve an overall pass, or if you have to achieve a pass in a set number of stations. For this OSCE you would have to pass both stations to be successful.

The OSCE

Adult basic life support OSCE station
Student information
IMPORTANT – PLEASE READ CAREFULLY

You are a first-year nursing student visiting a 45-year-old man with mild learning disabilities at his home with a member of the community nursing team. The nurse has popped out to the car to collect some equipment and receives a phone call at the same time. She is currently in her car on the phone. The patient is in the kitchen making you and your mentor a cup of tea. You are waiting in the sitting room when you hear a loud bang from the kitchen; you go to see what has happened. When you enter the kitchen you see that the patient is motionless on the floor.

You are required to assess the patient and act appropriately upon your findings.

N.B. Please ask if you are unclear about what it is that you have to do.

The above is the scenario attached to this OSCE. It may be that you have just been told that you will be assessed on your basic life support skills and knowledge and you have not been given the scenario until just prior to your OSCE, or you may have been given this scenario previously along with other information about the OSCE.

It does not really matter when you are given this information. The important thing is that you unpick it so that you are clear about what you are being asked to do. Therefore, read the scanario very carefully. If you are unclear about the scenario or any accompanying instructions, get clarification from the examiner. Do not feel embarrassed or worried about annoying the examiner – it is better to ask than to perform incorrectly at the station.

Below is the same scenario but we have identified the key points in order to help you understand what you are being asked to do.

Adult basic life support OSCE station

▲ *This tells you that you are being assessed on your basic life support skills on an adult patient. Therefore, in order to be successful you will need to perform the skills required in basic life support. You should have been given a skills session in this and also some reading materials and resources such as DVDs or websites. Your preparation prior to the OSCE would have been to revisit these.*

Student information

IMPORTANT – PLEASE READ CAREFULLY

▲ *This is telling you to read what follows as there will be some very important information within this section which will not only tell you what you are required to do but will provide you with relevant information to help you succeed in your OSCE.*

You are a first-year nursing student visiting a 45-year-old man with mild learning disabilities at his home with a member of the community nursing team.

▲ *This informs you of the setting and the age of the patient. This is very important in this scenario as you will not have any resuscitation equipment that would be available in an acute hospital setting; thus when you call for help you will need to call 999 for an ambulance rather than 2222 for the hospital resuscitation team. This may lead you to ask questions such as whether there will be a phone available in the examination room or whether you just have to inform the examiner that you are calling 999 and let them know what you would say.*

The nurse has popped out to the car to collect some equipment and receives a phone call at the same time. She is currently in her car on the phone.

> *This is telling you that you are on your own and should not expect the nurse to come back during the OSCE! The rationale for this is that the purpose of this OSCE is to assess your competence in resuscitation.*

The patient is in the kitchen making you and your mentor a cup of tea. You are waiting in the sitting room when you hear a loud bang from the kitchen; you go to see what has happened. When you enter the kitchen you see that the patient is motionless on the floor.

> *This informs you where the patient is and that you have to respond. As you did not witness the event and due to the fact that the patient is in the kitchen, the examiner will be expecting you to assess for danger prior to assessing the patient. If you remember, the first part of the Resuscitation Council algorithm for basic life support is 'D' for danger. Therefore you need to assess if it is safe to approach the patient.*

You are required to assess the patient and act appropriately upon your findings.

> *This is informing you that you need to continue with a systematic assessment of the Resuscitation Council algorithm DRSABC: 'danger', 'responsive', 'shout', 'airway', 'breathing' and 'circulation', and act appropriately according to your findings. For example, if you find that your patient is unresponsive and has no signs of life, you will need to commence CPR. If you have not already been informed you will need to ascertain whether you will using a basic manikin, in which case you will need to ask the examiner what your findings are, or whether you be using an advanced manikin where breathing can be assessed directly by you.*

N.B. Please ask if you are unclear about what it is that you have to do.

> *This is giving you permission to ask questions!*

OSCE checklist

Table 6.1 is the checklist that could be used at this station. You will see that it is divided into 'skill', 'criteria', 'achieved' and 'comments'. The skills that you are being assessed on will be under the 'skill' column. The 'criteria' column splits the skill into sections and therefore helps you understand the level of performance you are expected to achieve.

You should have carried out these skills under supervision in a simulated practice session, however, it is important that you revisit these skills. If you are unsure of your level of skill you need to seek support from your tutor. Once again we have annotated the criteria in the checklist to help you gain greater understanding of the skills you would be required to demonstrate in this OSCE.

If you annotate your OSCE checklist in a similar way, it will provide you with a better understanding of what skills you need to perform and why. It is very important that not only can you perform each element of the skill correctly but also that you understand *why* they should be performed in this way. Therefore we suggest that you write against each criterion why it is important and include the evidence base behind it.

This level of understanding is very important so that you can apply the principles to different clinical situations and hence practise safely. In this checklist (Table 6.1) you are asked first to 'assess danger' and the rationale behind this is that you need to do an initial risk assessment and ensure it is safe to approach the patient; also that you are not putting yourself at risk. This is a very good example of the need to know *why* you are doing something and not just *how* to complete the task!

You will see that this OSCE checklist does not have bold criteria. It is therefore important that you find out what the consequences would be should you miss out a component.

You will see that at the end of the checklist it states:

All criteria have to be attempted using a systematic approach conforming with the Resuscitation Council basic life support algorithm in order to pass the OSCE. If any criteria is not attempted, attempted but performed incorrectly or not to an appropriate standard the student will fail the OSCE.

This tells you that you are required to perform every criterion to the required standard in order to pass the OSCE.

The comments box will allow the examiner to provide you with written feedback on your performance. This could be in the form of congratulating you on your performance or giving you constructive feedback so that you know where

Table 6.1 Adult basic life support OSCE checklist

Skill	Criteria	Achieved		Comments
		Yes	No	
(D) Assess **danger**	Assesses if it is safe to approach the patient *You need to make it very explicit that you are assessing the area for danger prior to approaching the patient. You should inform the examiner that you are assessing for danger and what types of danger you are looking for. This needs to be related to the location of the incident, in this case the kitchen. You could include looking for electrical cables, water, spilt oil, etc. Remember the examiner cannot read your mind so you need to narrate your way through your actions in the OSCE, informing the examiner of what you are doing.*			
(R) Check **response**	Checks for response by: • Calling the patient's name • Tapping the patient on the shoulder and calling his/her name *In this section you are checking if the patient is responsive and therefore their level of consciousness. The most effective way to do this is by calling the patient's name. If they do not respond then incorporate touch as a stimulant as well as speech. If you do not get any response you can deduce that you have a patient who is unconscious and therefore you need to act accordingly.*			
(S) Shout for help	Calls out, asking for help *Here you are calling for help as you have found that you have a patient who is unresponsive and will need some sort of help. You are hoping that the nurse who is with you will hear you or perhaps a passer-by or neighbour.*			

(A) Assess airway	Checks if the airway is clear			
	Part of assessing the airway is to find out if there is anything obvious blocking the airway that could be easily removed. You are also looking for anything that could potentially obstruct the airway further when you open the airway.			
	Opens airway using a head tilt, chin lift manoeuvre			
	You need to open the airway to give the patient every opportunity to breathe. Head tilt, chin lift is the manoeuvre used and this section is assessing whether you are able to perform this skill correctly.			
(B) Breathing and (C) circulation	Checks for breathing and signs of life for not more than 10 seconds by: • Looking • Listening and • Feeling			
	In this section you need to be able to show that you know how to check for the above. You need to tell the examiner that you are looking, listening and feeling and what you are looking and feeling for. Do you know how to check for breathing and signs of life? What does 'look, listen and feel' mean in this context? You could write notes on your checklist to remind you of what you need to do in order to achieve these three elements.			
Ensure help is coming/ get help	Calls 999 and provides accurate and concise information			
	Here you will need to accurately state where you are and what the problem is. Try practising this so that it does not feel so awkward when you do it.			
Commence compressions	Correct hand position: heel of your hand in the centre of the chest with the other hand on top			

(Continued)

Skill	Criteria	Achieved		Comments
		Yes	No	
	30 compressions delivered at: • A rate of 100/min • A depth of 4–5cm *Here you are being assessed on the accuracy of your compressions. You have to:* • *know the correct hand position;* • *complete the correct amount of compressions at the correct rate and depth.* *This checklist has provided you with this information, however if it did not you could add this to your notes.*			
Commence two breaths	Attempts two breaths by: • Opening airway using a head tilt, chin lift technique • Using a pocket mask to blow into the mouth • Watches for chest to rise and fall *Once again you are being asked to demonstrate your skills of opening the airway but this time you also need to demonstrate that you can use a pocket mask correctly and give two effective breaths.*			
Continue with effective CPR	Continues with chest compressions and breaths using a ratio of 30:2 until either help arrives or asked to stop *This tells you need to continue with CPR until you are informed by the examiner to stop.*			

Note: All criteria have to be attempted using a systematic approach conforming with the Resuscitation Council basic life support algorithm in order to pass the OSCE. If any criteria is not attempted, attempted but performed incorrectly or not to an appropriate standard the student will fail the OSCE.

to improve. For example, the examiner may say, 'Ensure your compressions are continually at a rate of 100 per minute; occasionally you were too fast.'

Chapter 7 will provide you with further guidance on how to make best use of the feedback given to you by your examiner.

Pass/fail

Having 'pass/fail' informs you that you will either pass or fail the OSCE and will not be given a grade. You need to ensure that you find out what are the consequences of failing the OSCE: will you be offered another attempt or will you have to take this part of the course again?

Station two: multiple choice questions

Station two is a multiple choice paper that assesses the knowledge related to the skill that you performed in station one. If your OSCE is a series of stations, the multiple choice could assess your knowledge related to all the stations rather than just one. This station is an objective test as the answers are predetermined and selected by you from a number of alternatives.

The multiple choice consists of three elements:

- the 'stem' containing the problem or statement;
- the 'key' which is the correct response; and
- 'distractors', or 'incorrect' responses.

This type of test is very versatile in that it can measure a variety of levels of functioning. The example below assesses your level of knowledge related to the management of basic life support.

Try to answer each question to test your own knowledge before looking at the answers.

1 There are several things you need to do when you encounter a person in need of assistance. What should you do first?
    a) Determine responsiveness
    b) Check for danger
    c) Call for help
    d) Commence CPR

2 Is it advisable to check for signs of circulation in adults by finding the carotid pulse?
    a) No
    b) Yes

3 'No signs of life' means:
    a) Unconscious, unresponsive, not moving and not breathing normally
    b) Has no pulse
    c) Unconscious, unresponsive and not moving

4 Which of these means would be appropriate to 'open the airway' of a child victim?
   a) Maintain head in neutral position
   b) Backward head tilt and chin lift

5 Which of these terms means 'CPR'?
   a) The technique of rescue breathing combined with chest compressions
   b) Basic life support

6 When you commence CPR, how many initial breaths would you give?
   a) 2
   b) 3
   c) 5

7 Another way of looking at the rate of compression is:
   a) The number of compressions given between breathing
   b) The number of compressions given in a minute

8 What is the recommended rate of compressions?
   a) 100 compressions per minute
   b) 30 compressions per minute

9 What is the recommended ratio of compressions to breaths?
   a) 100 compressions to two breaths
   b) 30 compressions to two minutes
   c) 30 compressions to two breaths

10 The recommended ratio of compressions to breathing (30:2) applies to:
   a) Adults
   b) Younger children
   c) Older children
   d) Infants
   e) All of these

11 Do you need to count the number of cycles per minute when giving CPR?
   a) Yes
   b) No

12 What is the recommended way to determine the location point for chest compressions?
   a) Place two fingers at the point where the lower ribs meet, then place your other hand next to that
   b) Find the centre of the chest (lower half of the sternum)

13 What method of compression should you use for infants?
   a) The two finger technique
   b) The heel of one hand with the other hand firmly on top of the lower hand

Answers

1. b 2. a 3. c 4. a 5. a 6. a 7. b 8. a 9. c 10. a 11. b 12. b 13. a

OSCE example 2: medicines management

Explanation

The purpose of this OSCE is to assess your knowledge and skill in relation to medicines management and assesses the ESCs related to safe medicines management. This OSCE would be suitable for a pre-registration nursing student in their final year of study. The key areas assessed are as follows:

- The principles of pharmacodynamics and pharmacokinetics, identifying factors that may influence this process (e.g. extremes of life, disease processes).
- Rationale for decision-making in administration in relation to drug dosages for minimal side-effects, interactions and hypersensitivity.
- Awareness of the professional accountability of the nurse and legal and ethical implications.
- Ability to reflect upon practice experiences and demonstrate application of theory to practice.
- Effective decision-making in medicines administration.
- Knowledge of the identification of the role of the nurse and other health care professionals in medicines administration and client education.

The examination consists of one station with the following timings:

- 10-minute preparation and reading (a BNF will be provided);
- 15-minute medication administration;
- 5-minute questioning, which consists of the examiner asking the student a maximum of *three questions* pertinent to the case scenario and medication regime as indicated on the examination sheet.

Therefore, the total time allowed for this OSCE is 30 minutes.
   The examiner will also act as the staff nurse supervising the student on the ward and will therefore act as the second checker following the administration of any medication.

The OSCE

Medicines management OSCE station
Student information
IMPORTANT – PLEASE READ CAREFULLY

Sasha Kera has been living in a care home for two years following an ischemic stroke. Sasha is due to receive her medication. It is 0800hrs: please administer her morning medications as outlined on the drug chart:

Ramipril 10mg od at 08.00hrs

Aspirin 75mg od at 08.00hrs

Dipyridamole MR 200 mg bd at 08.00hrs and 20.00hrs

You have 10 minutes prior to your OSCE commencing. In this time you are able to utilize the BNF to ensure you have the adequate knowledge to administer these medications according to the NMC *Standards for Medicines Management* (NMC 2008b).

For this OSCE, although you are aware that the skill you will be carrying out will be medicines management, it is not until you arrive that you are given the scenario. Therefore your preparation would be to learn the *process* for administration of medication. You would then be able to use the BNF to support you in being aware of the therapeutic usage and contraindication of the medication you are required to administer.

In the explanation section it states that you will be given 10 minutes reading time, and you need to use these 10 minutes wisely and review the drugs in the BNF to ensure that you are aware of why the patient is taking the medication and common side-effects and contraindications.

Below is the same scenario with the key points identified to help you understand what you are being asked to do, and the main points you need to jot down in relation to the drugs you will administer.

Medicines management station
Student information

IMPORTANT – PLEASE READ CAREFULLY

Sasha Kera has been living in a care home for two years following an ischemic stroke. Sasha is due to receive her medication. It is 08.00hrs: please administer her morning medications as outlined on the drug chart:

You may feel that you do not have enough information about the patient's condition, however, if the examiners thought you needed more information they would have given it to you! Think about the medication that you have been asked to administer and the respective therapeutic uses: this will help you understand why the patient has been prescribed these medications. You could confirm this with the patient themselves during the OSCE.

You are being asked to administer Sasha's 08.00 medication. However, in order to do this safely you need to be aware of polypharmacy (the interaction of drugs) and hence you need to consider what other medication she is on. This will be on the chart, therefore the key here is to review the medication chart as a whole and not just the 08.00 medication. You need to ensure you are aware of the following in relation to each of the prescribed medications:

- *therapeutic usage;*
- *normal dosage;*
- *common side-effects;*
- *precautions;*
- *contraindications.*

You can gain all of this information from the BNF. The examiner is looking for your ability to analyse the information and utilize the information relevant for Sasha, as many drugs have more than one therapeutic usage and dosages are often determined by the usage. We have completed this for the drug ramipril as an example – try carrying out the same task for the other prescribed medications.

Ramipril 10mg od at 08.00hrs

Therapeutic usage: ramipril is an angiotensin-converting enzyme inhibitor (ACE inhibitor). One of its common uses is to treat mild to moderate hypertension and prevention of stroke. Hypertension could have been one of the contributing factors towards the stroke that Sasha suffered two years ago. Therefore you could conclude that this is why Sasha has been prescribed ramipril. Normal dosage for prophylaxis of stroke is 10mg od (once per 24 hours). As Sasha is prescribed 10mgs od you can conclude that she is taking a correct dose. However, you may wish to check what her blood pressure is to determine its effectiveness. Common side-effects of this drug include profound hypotension, renal impairment and a persistent dry cough. You need to ensure that the patient is aware of this and what they should do if they are suffering from any of these side-effects. For example, with profound hypotension they may get dizzy when standing up too quickly. Precautions include hypotension with the first doses, which should be initiated with care with patients receiving diuretics. ACE inhibitors should also be used with caution in peripheral vascular disease. You can see that Sasha is not on diuretics, and you should be able to ascertain from the notes or the examiner how long she has been on the medication and whether she has peripheral vascular disease. Contraindications include patients with hypersensitivity to ACE inhibitors. ACE inhibitors should not be used in pregnancy. Checking if Sasha has any allergies will inform you if she has sensitivity to ACE inhibitors.

Aspirin 75mg od at 08.00hrs

Dipyridamole MR 200 mg bd at 08.00hrs and 20.00hrs

You have 10 minutes prior to your OSCE commencing. In this time you are able to utilize the BNF to ensure you have the adequate knowledge to administer these medications according to the NMC *Standards for Medicines Management* (NMC 2008b).

This is giving you permission to utilize the BNF so you are sure that you are aware of the therapeutic usage, normal dosages, common side-effects, precautions and contraindications of all of Sasha's medications (not just the 08.00hrs medications). As per the NMC Standards for Medicines Management *you must know the therapeutic uses of the medicine to be administered, its normal dosage, side-effects, precautions and contraindications in order to be able to meet the set standards. However, no one can be expected to know this about every drug, therefore it is safe practice to use the BNF to support you in this. What many practitioners aim to know are the normal dos-*

ages, side-effects, precautions and contraindications of drug groups – for example, steroids, anti-hypertensives, beta blockers and simple analgesics.

A point of caution: ensure that when you verbalize this information to the patient you use lay terms and not medical jargon – you do not want to confuse or frighten them. You should only discuss the most common side-effects with the patient, so they can make an informed decision regarding taking or not taking the medication.

Ask the examiner if you are able to make notes about the drugs and take these into the OSCE with you, and ask also whether there will be a BNF available in the OSCE.

Table 6.2 is an example of a checklist that could be used for this OSCE. Here, the bold criteria are mandatory to pass the exam. Failure of one mandatory aspect will result in you receiving a technical fail, even if your overall mark is above the pass mark. This is because you will not have been deemed competent.

If you look closely at the bold criteria, you will see that they correlate to the standards set by the NMC for medicines management which can be found at the following link: www.nmc-uk.org/aArticle.aspx?ArticleID=3958. Consequently, you would be strongly advised to view a copy of these standards to help you prepare for this OSCE.

If you demonstrate all of the mandatory criteria to a satisfactory standard, the OSCE mark is calculated by adding the scores you receive in each section to give an overall percentage mark.

Table 6.2 OSCE checklist for medicines management

Activity	Performance expected	Refer	Satisfactory	Good	Excellent
Professional behaviour *This will be assessed throughout the OSCE and relates to the NMC Code and ESCs*	• Adheres to school dress code	0	1	2	2
	• **Behaves in a professional manner respecting others, adopting non-discriminatory behaviour**	–2	2	3	4
	• **Demonstrates professionalism through approach to practice**	–2	2	3	4

(Continued)

Activity	Performance expected	Refer	Satisfactory	Good	Excellent
Communication skills	• Introduces self, giving name	0	1	2	3
	• Asks what patient would like to be called	0	1	2	3
	• Good eye contact, appropriate use of touch and clarity of voice	0	1	2	3
	• Uses open questions	0	1	2	3
	• Offers patient opportunity to ask questions and gives clear answers	0	2	4	4
	• **Checks patient identity: verbally, ID bracelet and prescription chart**	–2	1	2	2
	• **Gains informed consent for administration of medication**	–2	2	2	6
	The first part of this section is assessing the finer communication skills. It is about building a rapport with your patient. Establishing a rapport in the early part of the OSCE sets the scene for the rest of the exam. It is done simply by greeting the patient warmly and giving a clear introduction including your name, role and purpose: for example, 'I am Susan, a third-year nursing student and I have been asked to administer your morning medication with the support of my mentor.' You will then need to inform the patient of what this involves in order for you to gain an informed consent from them.				
	Taking your time carrying out a good introduction will buy you time to compose yourself and gather your thoughts before you move on with the task. A word of advice: students that dive straight in often make silly mistakes!				

Procedure	• Consults prescription chart to ascertain drugs, dose, timing, route, method of administration and doctor's signature	–2	2	4	6
	• Assesses patient as necessary (identifying specific observations that need to be carried out prior to administration)	–2	2	4	6
	• Informs patient of medication to be administered	–2	2	4	6
	• Checks patient's understanding, offers explanations as needed and answers any questions	0	2	3	4
	• Considers benefits of written information as support	0	2	3	4
	• Checks for allergies, verbally and on prescription chart	–2	2	3	4
	• Selects required medication, checks name, strength and expiry date (verbalizes action)	–2	2	3	4
	• Offers glass of water	0	1	2	2
	• Ensures patient has taken medication (verbalizes action)	–2	1	2	3
	• Makes a clear, accurate and immediate record of medication administered	–2	2	3	4
	• Obtains counter-signature of examiner	–2	1	2	3
	• Returns environment to previous state	0	1	2	2

(Continued)

Activity	Performance expected	Refer	Satisfactory	Good	Excellent
	During the procedure you will need to carry out each step to an appropriate standard. Therefore it is important to ensure that you can memorize each of these steps so that they are second nature to you when it comes to the OSCE. Remember to talk aloud, stating what you are doing so that the examiner does not miss anything when they are looking down the marking criteria. For example, when you are reviewing the drug chart read aloud:				
	• the name of the medication;				
	• the dose of the medication; *• the formulation of the medication;*				
	Check that the chart is dated, timed and signed by the prescriber. Verbalize what the drugs are for, whether the dosages are within the therapeutic range, and so on. The terminology that you use to explain this to the patient will need to be in lay terms. However, explaining them in more detail to the examiner separately will demonstrate a greater depth of knowledge base and hence increase your mark.				
Knowledge base	**• Is able to articulate legal and ethical duties in relation to medication administration**	–2	2	4	6
	• Verbalizes therapeutic uses and normal doses of prescribed medication	–2	2	4	6

	• **Verbalizes side-effects, cautions and contraindications of prescribed medication**	–2	2	4	6
	These are the questions the examiner will ask if you do not cover them during the OSCE. It is better to offer this information voluntarily than wait to be questioned.				

Assessment criteria

Table 6.3 is an example of an assessment marking criteria that will help you determine what your performance would need to be in order to achieve specific grades. You will see that the OSCE marking criteria is divided into four elements. If you are offered assessment criteria as well as a checklist you should use this to help you increase your score/mark.

You will see that in order to achieve 90–100 per cent you need to deliver a near perfect performance and have a broad, detailed and accurate knowledge base. Take time to read the criteria and the checklist.

Table 6.3 Assessment marking criteria

Assessment criteria student number: **Date:**

Grade	Professional behaviour	Communication skills	Procedure	Knowledge base
A: 90–100% Almost no room for improvement at this level	Excellent and consistent professional behaviour. Uniform worn according to Code.	Gives clear, concise and precise verbal instructions and full explanations to patient. Checks understanding throughout the procedure. Gives reassurance to promote concordance.	Safe in all aspects of procedure. Confident, fluent technique with rationale.	Demonstration of a broad, detailed and accurate knowledge of all aspects of relevant underpinning theory. Applies knowledge to scenario to offer sound clinical decision-making and assessment.

(Continued)

Grade	Professional behaviour	Communication skills	Procedure	Knowledge base
A: 80–89% Exceptionally high level of performance.	Excellent and consistent professional behaviour. Uniform worn according to Code.	Gives clear, concise and precise verbal instructions and full explanations to patient and checks understanding throughout the procedure. Gives reassurance to promote concordance.	Safe in all aspects of procedure. Confident, fluent technique with rationale.	Demonstration of a broad, detailed and accurate knowledge of all aspects of relevant underpinning theory. Considers assessment of scenario to support clinical decision-making and assessment.
A: 70–79% Excellent performance	Excellent and consistent professional behaviour. Uniform worn according to Code.	Gives clear, concise and precise verbal instructions and full explanations to patient. Checks understanding. Gives reassurance to promote concordance.	Safe in all aspects of procedure. Confident, fluent technique with rationale.	Demonstration of a detailed and accurate knowledge of key aspects of relevant underpinning theory. Considers assessment of scenario to support clinical decision-making and assessment.
B+: 60–69% Very good performance	Appropriate clothing and identification, some aspects of uniform code omitted. Professional approach throughout.	Gives clear and precise verbal instructions and explanations to patient. Checks understanding. Gives reassurance and explanation to promote concordance.	Safe in all aspects of procedure. Could extend role to promote concord-ance.	Demonstration of an accurate knowledge of key aspects of relevant underpinning theory. Considers assessment of most elements of the scenario but not fully applied.

B: 50–59% Good performance	Appropriate clothing and identification, some aspects of uniform code omitted. Approaches task in professional manner.	Gives clear verbal instructions and explanations to patient without prompting.	Safe in all aspects of procedure. Could extend role to promote concord-ance.	Demonstration of knowledge of key aspects of relevant underpinning theory with minor inaccuracies.
C: 41–49% Acceptable performance	Acceptable clothing. Demonstrates awareness of professional behaviour.	Gives satisfactory verbal instructions and explanations to patient with minimal prompting.	Safe in all aspects of procedure. Could extend role to promote concord-ance. May lack organiza-tion.	Demonstration of knowledge of key aspects of relevant underpinning theory with minor inaccuracies and needing some prompting through questioning.
D: 40% Only just satisfactory	Acceptable clothing, some awareness of behaviour in reflection.	Gives verbal instructions to patient; needs prompting; acceptable summary. Some awareness of communica-tion in reflection.	Safe in all aspects of procedure; demon-strates limited awareness of role in reflection.	Demonstration of some knowledge of key aspects of relevant underpinning theory with minor inaccuracies and needing prompting through questioning.
Resit: **30–39%** Weak performance. Failure of one or more essential criteria.	Little awareness or insight.	Unclear instructions and explanations given to patient. Lacks understanding of the significance of effective communication.	Unsafe in one or more aspect of procedure. Little awareness. Inaccurate and ineffective application of the skill.	Limited and inaccurate knowledge of key aspects of relevant underpinning theory. Unsafe application of theory to practice.

(Continued)

Grade	Professional behaviour	Communication skills	Procedure	Knowledge base
Fail: 0–29% Generally weak performance. Failure of one or more criteria.	Unprofessional and careless approach.	Unclear and imprecise verbal instructions and explanations given to patient.	Unsafe in one or more aspects of procedure. Inadequate insight on reflection. Inaccurate and ineffective application of the skill.	Insufficient and inaccurate knowledge of key aspects of relevant underpinning theory. Unsafe application of theory to practice.

OSCE example 3: aseptic non-touch technique

Explanation

The purpose of this OSCE is to assess your knowledge and skill in relation to aseptic non-touch technique (also known as ANTT). This OSCE would be suitable for a pre-registration nursing student in any year of their study and assesses the following broad aspects:

- ability to prepare the patient and the appropriate equipment for ANTT;
- ability to demonstrate how ANTT is performed.

The OSCE

Aseptic non-touch technique OSCE station
Student information
IMPORTANT – PLEASE READ CAREFULLY

Richard May, aged 72, was admitted to your ward for rehabilitation following a myocardial infarction. He had a small non-cancerous lesion removed from his arm three days ago and the dressing requires changing. Under the direct supervision of your mentor, you are going to remove the current dressing and clean and redress the wound using ANTT.

This could be a stand-alone OSCE or a station during an OSCE circuit. From the scenario and the checklist (Table 6.4), you may think at first that you are being assessed on your skills only. However, these are generic principles of wound dressing using ANTT which have been turned into an OSCE checklist. In order to apply these to the scenario you will need a certain level of knowledge related to preventing cross-infection, aseptic technique and ANTT.

Your knowledge related to ANTT and infection control may be assessed further in an alternative way – for example, an exam paper, short answer questions or an essay. This is a pass/fail OSCE, therefore no mark is awarded. However, if your pass/fail is graded you can tell if you have passed well (good) or only just passed (borderline pass).

The examiner will give a global rating on how you perform your skills in relation to:

- attention to detail;
- organization;
- articulation when required to give information;
- engagement and reception to cues;
- professional presentation;
- engagement with the patient.

If you look at the checklist you will see that it is underpinned by evidence-based practice in relation to preventing cross-infection and the principles of ANTT. You therefore need to learn each of the steps of this procedure, ensuring that you understand the underlying principles of ANTT. This is essential for you to be able to adapt the guidelines to the scenario that you have been given.

The important principle here is that when ANTT is applied to wound dressings the open wound should not come into contact with any item that is not sterile, and any items that have been in contact with the wound must be discarded safely or decontaminated.

Using the same principles applied to the previous two OSCE examples, try and complete the student information and the checklist and answer the following questions:

- What are you being asked to do?
- What key information can you gain from the student information that will help you during your OSCE?
- What is each criterion asking you to do?
- What is the underpinning knowledge?
- Do you have the underpinning knowledge?

- If not, how and where can you obtain it?
- Can you perform the skill correctly?
- If so, how would you grade yourself?

Table 6.4 OSCE checklist for principles of ANTT

Step	Criterion	Achieved	Not achieved
Preparation of patient	Seeks patient's permission/consent to perform the procedure *Your response:*		
	Checks patient is comfortable and in good position *Your response:*		
	Adjusts patient's clothing to expose wound area while respecting patient dignity *Your response:*		
Preparation of health care professional	Washes hands using all stages of the National Patient Safety Agency (NSPA) hand-cleaning technique *Your response:*		
	Uses lever-operated taps/infra-red taps correctly *Your response:*		
	Using hand towels and working from fingertips towards the wrists, dries hands and wrists effectively without re-contaminating themselves *Your response:*		

	Disposes of hand towels using foot-operated waste bin		
	Puts on plastic apron		
	Your response:		
	Places yellow clinical waste bag in an accessible position near to the patient		
	Your response:		
Preparation of equipment	Puts on a plastic apron		
	Your response:		
	Cleans dressing trolley/dressing tray		
	Your response:		
	Assembles all equipment needed for the procedure and checks integrity and expiry dates of all sterile items		
	Your response:		
	Opens dressing pack using the four corners of the paper and avoiding sterile inner surfaces and content		
	Your response:		
	Prepares sterile field		
	Your response:		
	Opens sachet of normal saline and opens any additional equipment onto the sterile field		
	Your response:		

(Continued)

Step	Criterion	Achieved	Not achieved
Dressing procedure	Puts on a pair of clean vinyl/latex gloves *Your response:*		
	Removes old dressing and disposes of this appropriately *Your response:*		
	Removes vinyl/latex gloves and disposes of these appropriately *Your response:*		
	Decontaminates hands with alcohol hand rub using all stages of the NSPA hand-cleaning technique *Your response:*		
	Puts on sterile gloves using appropriate technique in order to maintain asepsis *Your response:*		
	Uses a gloved hand, gauze and warmed normal saline solution to clean around edges of wound *Your response:*		
	Uses a gloved hand and gauze to dry wound edges *Your response:*		
	Avoids contamination of sterile field and wound site *Your response:*		

	Disposes of swabs appropriately *Your response:*		
	Applies non-adhesive dressing as appropriate, ensuring it is secure *Your response:*		
	Removes gloves and apron and disposes of them correctly *Your response:*		
	Seals disposal bag before leaving patient *Your response:*		
	Maintains patient's privacy and dignity throughout procedure *Your response:*		
	Disposes of all clinical waste according to local infection control policy (yellow clinical waste bag) *Your response:*		
	Decontaminates hands with alcohol hand rub using all stages of the NSPA hand-cleaning technique *Your response:*		

Examiner global rating

Good	Pass	Borderline pass	Borderline fail	Fail

Examiner's comments

Write in here how you think you did!

How did you get on? Was it as easy as you expected or do you need to do more preparation to pass this OSCE?

Chapter 7 will give you an understanding of what makes a good performance in an OSCE. It will also detail what good feedback contains and help you to appreciate how this feedback can empower you to improve your practice. You will start to recognize the development of self-assessment through reflection.

Chapter summary

1 Fully read any documentation or guidelines given to you before the OSCE.

2 Set yourself a date when you can sit down and work through the documentation. You could do this on your own or with your peers.

3 Ensure you have an understanding of the complexities of your OSCE.

4 Ensure you are fully aware of all the possible components of the OSCE assessment that you may be exposed to.

5 Ensure you are aware of the minimum standard of competency you will have to demonstrate to pass your OSCE and aim to achieve *above* this.

6 Examine your OSCE checklists and any marking criteria and make sure you read them thoroughly in order to understand the key components of your OSCE.

7 Identify any areas that seem unclear. These are the areas that you really need to clarify and understand before the OSCE, therefore ensure you ask for clarification from your tutor or examiner.

8 The OSCE checklist and marking criteria should be used to help you prepare and succeed in your OSCE.

9 Confirm whether the OSCE is pass/fail or has a grade attached to it.

10 The key to success is practice, practice and more practice.

After the OSCE has finished

7

Attitude is a little thing that makes a big difference.

Sir Winston Churchill (1874–1965)

By the end of this chapter you will:

○ Have an understanding of what makes a good performance in an OSCE.
○ Have an understanding of what good feedback contains.
○ Appreciate how this feedback can empower you to improve your practice.
○ Recognize the development of self-assessment through reflection.
○ Understand the process for the release of results following summative and formative assessments.

The importance of feedback cannot be underestimated in helping you to get the most out of your OSCE, and to create a sense of ownership in your own development. Feedback should be a two-way process where you feel that you are working in partnership with your tutor, and are not just a recipient of information about your progress. To help you to gain insight into your needs and show how you can use feedback most effectively, we have structured this chapter on a model that meets your needs as a learner. The model used is based on principles by Nicol and Macfarlane-Dick (2006). They synthesized research literature in the area of self-regulation and formative assessment, and identified seven principles of good feedback practice. These principles have been further adapted below by us to illustrate how you can use feedback to empower yourself and to develop yourself as an independent learner.

This chapter is therefore structured around the following seven key topics:

1   How to identify a good performance.
2   How to develop your skills for reflection.
3   Understanding the information you are given in feedback.

4   How to get the most from dialogue with your tutors.
5   Your motivational beliefs and self-esteem.
6   How to reduce the gap between your actual and ideal performance.
7   How you can contribute to evaluation.

How to identify a good performance

The most effective way to achieve your goal is to:

- understand what your goal is;
- take on ownership; and
- assess your own progress against that goal.

It probably seems obvious that it is best that your goals are also those of your tutors, however, research has shown that there is sometimes quite a gap between what your tutors are expecting of you and what you think you need to achieve (Hounsell 1997). In addition, Norton (1990) has shown that students have different ideas about goals and criteria for essays. We are concentrating on OSCEs in this book, but it is still important to be aware that your view of what you should be aiming for and your tutor's view may differ. Naturally, it is vital that you are both aiming for the *same* goal. This will ensure that there are no discrepancies between what you think you are being assessed against and the criteria on which you are actually being assessed.

> Sometimes there is a gap between what your tutors are expecting of you and what you think you need to achieve.

Rust *et al.* (2003) have shown, through research, that it is a difficult task to make assessment criteria and standards clear in written or even verbal descriptions. In this book we have aimed to explain the criteria you may be assessed on as clearly as possible, but your interpretation may still not be the same as ours! To help with this, we have given you examples in many chapters, along with detailed explanations about what is actually being looked for in each part of the OSCE. This approach is recommended by Orsmond *et al.* (2002). Yet it remains important for you to clarify verbally, in writing and by example from your tutors, *exactly* what is being looked for and assessed in your OSCE.

> Clarify verbally, in writing and by example from your tutors, *exactly* what is being looked for and assessed in your OSCE.

Other strategies that have helped to make the criteria, expected goals and standards clear include:

- using well-designed criteria sheets and clear definitions of performance;
- making time in class for discussion and reflection about criteria and levels of performance expected;
- using peer assessment so that students are used to giving feedback to others and identifying how they may perform themselves;
- giving students the opportunity to develop their own assessment criteria to experience the process of using such a marking tool (Nicol and Macfarlane-Dick 2006).

How to develop your skills for reflection

One of the aims of feedback is to prompt you to reflect on your performance following your OSCE. You may already be familiar with the concept of reflection and have used it to inform and improve your practice. The main principle when thinking about reflection, identified by Johns (2000), is to use a model to *guide* you in the process, rather than trying to fit your reflection into a model. Bulman writes that 'I see reflection as reviewing experience from practice so that it may be described, analysed, evaluated and consequently used to inform and change future practice' (Bulman and Schutz 2008: 2).

Reflection also takes courage. To make it meaningful you need to open up your practice to critiquing and examination by others as well as yourself. It is very tempting to reflect by yourself, but you may fall into the trap of not challenging yourself and engaging instead in self-affirmation, which is just seeing the OSCE from your angle and not thinking objectively. This may result in you not learning as much as you could have done from your reflection. Try to reflect with your peers so that you can challenge yourself and them. This will help you to develop the lifelong skill of accepting constructive criticism without feeling defensive. We will talk about this skill later in the chapter. Along with this you need a willingness to act on what you discover and an ability to change your practice. We have both found reflection to be a key component of our nursing careers and have used it constantly to inform and improve our work.

> Reflection also takes courage. To make it meaningful you need to open up your practice to critiquing and examination by others as well as yourself.

Professional development triangle

The professional development triangle, adapted from Jasper (2003), illustrates the role that reflection can have in informing professional practice. It is a useful tool to use as it enables you to see how, by undertaking learning with the OSCE activity, you can increase your knowledge and improve your practice (see Diagram 7.1).

If you use this triangle to reflect on an experience in an OSCE, such as hand-washing, you can see below how it can aid your performance (see Diagram 7.2).

There are a range of reflective models you could adopt to help you improve your practice. We have used the work of Gibbs *et al.* (1988) and Borton (1970) and have found their style of reflection particularly helpful. Below you will find an explanation of both models and examples of how they can be used to reflect on a hand-washing OSCE.

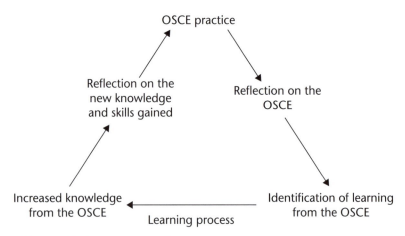

Diagram 7.1 Professional development triangle (adapted from Jasper 2003)

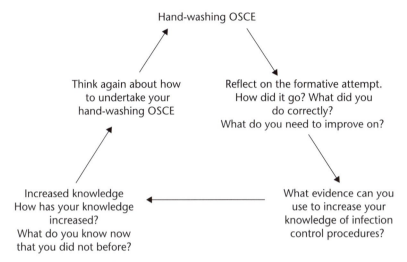

Hand-washing OSCE

Think again about how
to undertake your
hand-washing OSCE

Reflect on the formative attempt.
How did it go? What did you
do correctly?
What do you need to improve on?

Increased knowledge
How has your knowledge
increased?
What do you know now
that you did not before?

What evidence can you
use to increase your
knowledge of infection
control procedures?

Diagram 7.2 OSCE hand-washing development triangle

The Gibbs cycle

Gibbs *et al.* (1988) developed a cycle for structured debriefing and it is now used
by many people as a basis for their reflection. One key aspect of this work was
to value highly the need to analyse both feelings and events together as part of
the reflective process when thinking about practice. Table 7.1 takes you through
the stages of the cycle and is adapted from the Bulman and Schutz (2008) interpretation of it.

We have also developed an OSCE reflective cycle using adaptations from
Gibbs *et al.* (1988), Jasper (2003) and Bulman and Schutz (2008). This is shown
in Diagram 7.3 and gives you an illustration of how you can use reflection in
your OSCE. It helps you to see how you can think about reflection during the
OSCE process itself. You can then introduce analysis of your feelings and analysis of the literature to help you make sense of the OSCE. By this we mean using
your skills notes and any literature you have been recommended to review your
own knowledge base. The cycle then encourages you to think about what you
have learned that is new and how you can change your practice to improve in
the OSCE next time.

Table 7.1 Stages of the Gibbs cycle (adapted from Bulman and Schutz 2008)

Cycle	Interpretation of OSCE performance	Actual example of Jane undertaking a hand-washing OSCE
Description of the OSCE	Describe what happened during your OSCE. What did you do, how did you do it?	I had to undertake a formative hand-washing OSCE. I undertook this in a skills lab in our health care faculty. I was shown into the room and asked in my own time to undertake hand-washing. I was then asked a few questions by the tutor.
Feelings	How did you react during the OSCE? What feelings did you have while undertaking it? Just record these during this phase and don't think too deeply about them.	I was very nervous when I went into the room. It took me a while to get my bearings and I had to concentrate hard to understand what the tutor was saying to me. Although I had practised this OSCE it was very different doing it in exam conditions.
Evaluation of the OSCE	How did the experience make you feel and react? What was good and bad?	I think I did most parts of the hand-washing OK. Looking back on it, at one point I was not sure if I had washed my thumbs correctly and so I went back over these. I was also unsure about whether I had dried my hands correctly, so I made sure I redid this section too. I was very fazed by how nervous I felt and how the nerves made me forget a lot of the basic information I thought I knew.
Analysis of the OSCE	What evidence can you bring in from outside? Are there any themes that are apparent to you?	I chatted to colleagues afterwards and many of them had the same experiences. This was helpful and the colleagues who had done well were the ones who were very well prepared, so I must learn from this. I explained to my friends what I had done in the OSCE and asked them also how they thought I had done. I was starting to think I was better than I had been marked but they were able to really challenge me to think about the OSCE performance and not link the performance to me personally. This really helped me to think more objectively. Having looked at the seminar notes from this skills teaching session I now realize that I need

		to learn more about the reasons for correct hand-washing. This will help me to understand why I am doing things in a certain order and then hopefully make them easier to remember. The nerves were a part of my problem and so I think I need to make sure I am confident with my practice so that if I am nervous it will not affect me so much. It was really good to have gone through the formative attempt so that I now know what it will be like in the summative attempt and it won't be so daunting.
Conclusions for future practice	What have you learned in general from this experience?	I think I have now learned the value of being prepared and having a good knowledge base to understand why I am doing this in a particular way.
Conclusions specific for this OSCE	What specifics have you learned that can help you in particular?	I know that I react badly to nerves and so this has taught me to try and get on top of these so that I can be more productive and professional. This will also help me when I am out in a practice setting if I get nervous about doing something.
Action plan for future OSCEs	What will you do the same and what will you do differently in future?	I know that there were many aspects of the hand-washing I did OK in. However, I need to increase my knowledge base infection control and also develop strategies for managing my nerves, such as revision and being well prepared.

The Borton framework

A different type of technique to try is the Borton framework (1970). This revolves around three questions: 'What?', 'So what?' and 'Now what?' We have put this into an example for you (Table 7.2) so you can see how easily it can be used. Next to each question are trigger questions, although if you only remember the three main questions you will be doing very well.

- The 'What?' question is where you describe what happened in your OSCE.
- The 'So what?' question is the opportunity to review the OSCE more deeply and to analyse your feelings and knowledge base.
- The 'Now what?' question builds on the two previous questions and determines what you do in your next OSCE and how you can improve.

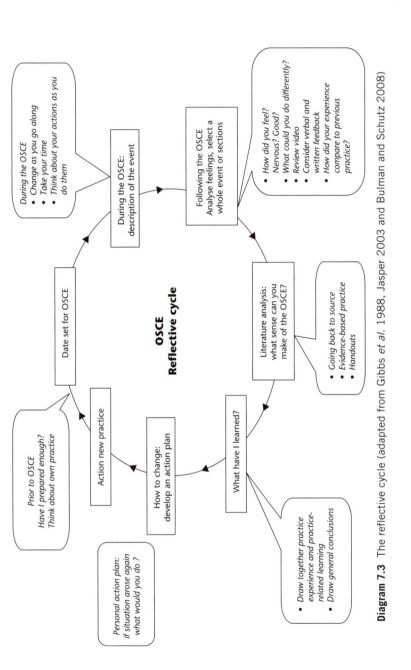

Diagram 7.3 The reflective cycle (adapted from Gibbs *et al.* 1988, Jasper 2003 and Bulman and Schutz 2008)

Table 7.2 Reflection based on Borton's (1970) framework

What? So what? Now what?	
What are you reflecting on?	I am going to reflect on my experience of the hand-washing OSCE that I have just completed.
What particular issues seem significant enough to demand attention?	Did I complete all six stages of hand-washing correctly? Did I dry my hands without recontaminating them?
What were others feeling and what made them feel that way?	I sensed that there were others undertaking their OSCE at the same time who were also very nervous.
What was I feeling and what made me feel that way?	I was feeling very nervous because of the examiner watching me.
What was I trying to achieve and did I respond effectively?	I was trying to achieve safe hand-washing and pass the OSCE.
What were the consequences of my actions on the patient, others and myself?	The consequences relate only to me in this instance as it was an examination. However, I recognize that in an actual practice setting the consequences of poor hand-washing will affect patients adversely.
So what factors influenced the way I was feeling, thinking and responding?	I was really wanting to make sure I undertook this correctly so that I am a safe practitioner. Not wanting to fail was making me nervous.
So what knowledge informed or might have informed me?	I had based my knowledge on the ESC related to infection prevention and control and the supporting literature that I was given as part of my skills practical session related to this area. I need to review all of this knowledge base before my next OSCE.
So to what extent did I act for the best?	I went into the OSCE as well prepared as possible as I felt I knew all the stages of hand-washing and drying.
So what, and how, does this situation connect with previous experiences?	Before I started my nursing course I had obviously washed my hands throughout my whole life. I had no idea, before undertaking practical sessions in the skills lab, how important it was to do this properly. I also had no idea about the risk to patients of not doing this properly.

(Continued)

What? So what? Now what?	
Now what might I do to respond more effectively given this situation again?	Although I felt fully prepared for this by ensuring that I could perform the skills, I had not recognized how my nerves could affect my performance.
Now what would the consequences of alternative actions for the patient, others and myself be?	If I fail this hand-washing OSCE and continue to fail I will not pass the course and will be a danger to my patients.
Now what do I feel about this experience?	I feel relieved that it is over, however, I am anxiously waiting my results and hope that I have shown safe practice.

You can reflect on your OSCE practice on the day of your assessment and then again once feedback is given to you (if you don't get your feedback immediately). In this way you can gain control of your reflection by undertaking it when *you* wish to, and gain from it what *you* need to. The important learning to take from the examples above is that reflection needs to work *for you*, therefore do try different models before opting for the one that suits you best. Have a look at Rolfe *et al.* (2001), Jasper (2003) and of course Bulman and Schutz (2008): they all show you exemplars, as well as taking you through a wider variety of models than we have been able to illustrate here.

Understanding the information you are given in feedback

You will receive feedback from peers and examiners following completion of your OSCE. Your tutors will be well versed in being able to identify any errors you have made. Your peers will be valuable in this area as well, and together they can help you to fully appreciate your strengths and areas for development. Freeman and Lewis (1998), among other authors, have identified that for feedback to be most effective it needs to be *timely* – for example, very close to your OSCE. It also needs to offer *constructive criticism* – for example, as well as explaining how you have made an error, it needs to ensure you understand how to rectify this.

> Feedback needs to be timely and occur soon after your OSCE to be most valuable.

As Wiggins (1998: 64) states, 'Feedback is not about praise or blame, approval or disapproval.' He recognizes the importance of feedback being given near to the event while the goals of the assessment are still fresh in the student's mind. Finally, feedback also needs to offer you praise for all the areas you managed well in your OSCE.

One of the key areas you can develop from your feedback is the ability to begin to *self-correct* and solve your problems proactively. To be able to do this, your feedback must be given to you in relation to the standards that are expected of you, either by use of a grading grid or clear goal standards.

Gibbs and Simpson (2004) have found that receiving regular feedback helps students to self-regulate more effectively. So if you are undertaking OSCE practice, ask for feedback often rather than just once. This should help you to progress more effectively and you should feel more in control of your progress. In addition, you may wish to prioritize your revision depending on the feedback from your OSCE. In this way you can focus on improvement where it is most needed.

> Ask for feedback regularly to improve your practice most effectively.

How to get the most from dialogue with your tutors

One of the comments made by students when they receive essays back is that the comments written on them do not make sense (Channock 2000; Hyland 2000). To make feedback effective and understandable, there needs to be a good dialogue between student and tutor. If you feel as though you are only being 'told' when getting the feedback from your OSCE, you may not play such an active role in understanding the messages being given. Your relationship with your tutor will be more effective if you view getting feedback on your OSCE as an opportunity to gain support but also to be challenged.

Pose some 'how' questions to yourself with your tutor and use these to try and guide your improvement:

- How do you think you did?
- How did you actually do?
- How can you improve?
- How can you do this?

A clear dialogue between student and tutor has been identified by Laurillard (2002) as essential if feedback is to be effective. So aim to have a discussion as mentioned above with your tutor about your OSCE performance, as well as reading the written feedback. Having a discussion will help you to get an immediate response to your queries as well as clearing up any misunderstandings you may have as to what has been written.

> Having a good dialogue with your tutor will help you to feel more of a partner in your feedback.

Think about how your feedback relates to the assessment criteria:

- you should always have the assessment criteria near when you are reviewing/receiving feedback as this is what the examiner would have assessed you against;
- if you do not understand your feedback or want further clarification or support in how to implement the suggestions, be prepared to ask the person who gave you the feedback for further advice, or support;
- feedback is a dialogue, so you should not be concerned about contacting the person and asking to meet up for further discussion;
- if you are receiving your feedback verbally, ensure you have a piece of paper and pen handy to write down key points mentioned by the examiner – this will ensure you have a paper copy to refer to at a later date;
- at the end of the feedback, ask to summarize your understanding of the feedback given, to ensure you have understood the examiner correctly.

Verbal feedback

Verbal feedback can also take place in a group setting, for example, watching a video-recording of an OSCE with your peers. In this case you will be able to get verbal feedback from your tutor as well as from your peers, who can also give a valuable perspective. Boyle and Nicol (2003) have identified the importance of peer feedback in terms of giving you more self-control over your learning. Often, discussing practice with fellow students will allow you to admit that you didn't know something either, which may be more difficult with your tutors. Hopefully, you will be really encouraged by your peers to improve *even more* as you are in the same boat as them! You could try using the 'How?' questions mentioned above with your peers and see what perspective they have on your OSCE.

> Listen to your fellow students and gain good feedback and encouragement to improve in your OSCE.

Your motivational beliefs and self-esteem

Your self-esteem and motivation will play a key role in your learning and what you can gain from an assessment such as an OSCE. It has been found that some students are less likely to read written comments if a grade is also given (Butler 1988). So try not to fall into this trap and if you have a grade, as well as written comments for your OSCE, make sure you read them fully. Although it is very tempting, try not to compare the grades that you receive with the ones of your fellow students. There will always be those who do better or less well than yourself. Comparing yourself to everyone else can make you less likely to think about your improvement and instead concentrate more on your performance in relation to others.

> Try not to compare your marks with others – concentrate instead on making your own performance better.

Responding to feedback

To be able to respond to feedback you need to have a certain level of self-awareness. Introspection is not sufficient for developing self-awareness: we also need pointers from other people such as peers and tutors. Being able to receive constructive feedback is an important interpersonal skill and a skill for life. If you receive negative feedback regarding an aspect of your behaviour or performance during the exam, it should be focused feedback on your specific performance. It should be constructive, without devaluing you as a person. This leads us to another area to work on, in the arena of self-esteem. Try to think of your feedback as a commentary on the *task* you undertook and *not you as a person*; aim to be objective and do not take your feedback too personally.

It is easy to be defensive when you receive feedback and it is useful to examine your own responses to feedback in different situations. Try doing this with a buddy: think of situations where you have both received feedback and then think about how you felt:

* Did you want to accept it?
* Did you feel 'hard done by?'
* Would you like to have reacted differently to the feedback?
* If so, how would you like to change?

You may wish to reflect on Dweck's (1999) observation that some students will have an 'entity view'. This means that they think there is a limit to what they can achieve, as opposed to students who have an 'incremental view'. These students believe that their ability can be flexible and will improve with effort and practice. If you are the 'entity view' person at the moment, you may feel that any failure is just an illustration of your low ability. So why not try to become an 'incremental view' person and think of OSCEs as a challenge? Then put real effort into making improvements.

> Work on being a person who sees themselves as someone who can always change and improve and does not have a fixed ability level.

How to reduce the gap between your actual and ideal performance

It is crucial that you feel:

- supported while you are undertaking the OSCE;
- supported through repeated practices at the OSCE;
- able to understand how to improve for your next OSCE as well as in clinical practice.

Support while you are undertaking the OSCE

Feedback comes in many formats, for example:

- written;
- verbal;
- comments made during the exam or while reviewing a recording of the exam;
- generic comments made during class feedback following the exam.

Feedback can come from:

- the examiners;
- seminar tutors;
- fellow students;
- the simulated patients themselves.

You may receive feedback in more than one format and at several points within the learning process, not just following the exam itself. In Table 7.3 you can see an example of feedback that could be given following a hand-washing OSCE.

Once you have received your feedback, ask yourself the following simple questions. If you do not know the answer to any of them, seek further guidance, in order to gain maximum benefit from the feedback.

1 Does the feedback identify what I have done well and what I need to improve on?
2 Can I see how this feedback will help me to plan future assessments?
3 Can I see how I can use this feedback to inform my practice?
4 Does this feedback help me to identify where I need to further develop my knowledge/understanding of the process being examined?

Table 7.3 Example of feedback from a hand-washing OSCE

Hand-washing	√ **Completes all stages of the National Patient Safety Agency (NSPA) hand-cleaning technique**
	√ **Uses lever-operated taps correctly**
	√ **Using hand towels, works from fingertips towards the wrists, dries hands and wrists effectively without re-contaminating themselves**
	√ **Disposes of hand towels using foot-operated waste bin**
	Well done, you have demonstrated safe hand-washing and drying technique. However, the following areas would improve your practice:
	• You need to perform the hand-washing in a timely manner, as it took you four minutes to complete the washing and drying. Although this was safe in practice you will need to speed up. The literature recommends that safe hand-washing and drying should take a minimum of 45 seconds and a maximum of 90 seconds.
	• Effective hand-drying is an important element. However, when drying your hands you need to think of resources and not use as many hand towels.
	It appeared that at one point the water had become too hot for you. Aim to make sure you have the water temperature correct for comfort before you start to wash your hands. Too hot will burn you and too cold will be ineffective.

Support through repeated practices at the OSCE

If you failed your OSCE, you need to be fully aware of what the consequences of this are. If the exam was formative (i.e. the purpose was to inform both you and your tutors of your current progress), then the result is important but not a final, as with a summative assessment. The important outcome is that you can identify for yourself what you did well and where you need to improve.

If your OSCE was summative (i.e. your final attempt), you need to find out if you will be given another chance, or if you have to retake any component of the course. It is essential that you find this information out prior to the OSCE. If you are unfortunate enough to fail the summative OSCE but you are offered another attempt, you need to ensure you seek tutorial advice and respond to the feedback that the examiner has given you.

Often the university will put on extra support sessions where you can either go and undertake practice in the simulated learning environment independently, or it is facilitated by one of the tutors. If this is offered, it is paramount that you attend. During these sessions you can clarify any feedback that you did not fully understand, and at the same time you can refine the skills that were identified as needing development, as well as receiving immediate feedback from the facilitator.

> Aim to attend any extra support sessions to gain the maximum amount of practice time for your OSCE.

Understanding how to improve for your next OSCE

If the OSCE is a formative attempt, the feedback will often be instant or very shortly after the OSCE. However, if it is summative, you may have to wait until the results have been ratified by an examination board. It is important that you get ready for your feedback. Find out what sort of feedback you can expect, when you can expect to receive it and who will be providing it. If this information is not explicit within the course/module documentation, then ask one of your tutors.

Your next step is to think about whether you are happy with the mark and the feedback. Are they what you were expecting? Were there any surprises? You then need to put an action plan into place to decide how you plan to respond to the feedback. It is tempting to only think about the comments or mark if you have not met the set criteria. However, it should not matter if you met the criteria, failed to meet the criteria or if the exam was formative or summative – you should still act upon the feedback.

> Put an action plan into place and highlight comments for future OSCEs.

A good place to start with your action plan is to highlight any comments that you feel would be useful in future OSCEs. For example, if during your OSCE you were asked to carry out an assessment of a patient's radial pulse and the examiner commented that your landmark for the radial pulse was incorrect, this would be a major error. In order to assess a patient's radial pulse safely, and hence meet essential criteria, you would need to be able to landmark the radial artery correctly. However, if one of the comments was that during your assessment you were very polite, but your voice was very quiet, this would be a minor error. The point is that you should be able to see where you have lost a lot of marks or even what caused you to fail to meet the essential criteria, as well as which minor errors could be worked on to improve future performances. Compare your list with previous feedback, not only for OSCEs but also feedback on your practice competencies:

- Are there any similarities?
- Can you see where you have improved?
- Can you see where you are not improving?
- If so, what do you need to do to improve?

Once you have completed your list:

- number the items in order of priority to help you plan your time effectively;
- consider how you are going to deal with each item on your list;
- consider how you are going to get further feedback. This may be from your tutor or from your peers.

You will also find it useful to think how you can improve your technique in your practice setting.

How you can contribute to evaluation

It is important to remember that your tutors need feedback on the OSCE process and your experience of it. You may be asked to give feedback via online questionnaires or as hard copy, as well as verbally. Tutors always aim to act on feedback given to them, in order to:

- improve the session for subsequent students;
- review their own performance;
- monitor quality for regulatory bodies, reports and visits.

Chapter summary

1 Find out when you can expect to receive feedback on your performance in the OSCE.

2 Find out in what format(s) you will receive your feedback.

3 Engage in your feedback, even if you passed.

4 Highlight any comments that you feel would be useful in future OSCEs.

5 Reflect on your performance and feedback given.

6 Aim to reflect with your peers to prevent you self-engaging in self-affirmation.

7 Act upon your reflection.

8 If you do not understand any of the feedback, ask for clarification.

9 If you fail your exam, ensure you seek support and take up any extra support that is offered.

10 Engage in evaluation of your OSCE process to help improve it for others.

Summary

8

In this chapter you will find all the tips, key points and useful subject summaries from throughout the book. We hope the chapter will prove a useful revision tool and quick reference guide for you.

1 Introducing OSCEs

Summary

- OSCE means Objective Structured Clinical Examination.
- This book will help you to:
  - understand your own learning style;
  - understand how reflection can give you greater understanding of your practice;
  - understand how you can be empowered to improve your practice.
- The teaching and assessment of clinical skills in a simulated learning environment have increased.
- There is a wide variety of simulated patients.
- There is a wide variety of simulated settings.
- Try to undertake a self-assessment of your current knowledge and skills.
- Self-assessment is a useful tool to master as it will enable you to develop the ability to examine and think critically about your practice.

Tips and key points

- OSCEs and practical examinations are a form of assessment which allows you to demonstrate your skills, knowledge and attitude.
- As with many new techniques, it is worth taking the time to practise and the more times you evaluate your practice, the easier the process will become.

2 Understanding OSCEs

Summary

Skills teaching, simulated learning and OSCEs:

- Are a rigorous way to identify your strengths and limitations.
- Will enable you to demonstrate your knowledge, skills and attitude in real-life health care situations.
- Can be undertaken in a clinical skills laboratory, computer-generated program or classroom.
- Will enable you to work through scenarios.
- Can give you instant feedback.
- Are well researched as a validated method of assessment.
- Allow you to practise and be examined in a safe environment.
- Are time-limited.
- Have quality assurance mechanisms built in.
- Will help you to be a more competent professional, learning in and from practice.

3 Preparing for your OSCE

Summary

- Ensure you take every opportunity possible to undergo supervised simulated practice so that you get used to the environment and equipment that will be used in your exam.
- Attend formative OSCEs and act upon the feedback that the examiners give you.
- Ensure you have the adequate level of knowledge and skills to undertake the OSCE by making use of lecture notes and other resources.
- Make use of any additional information the lecturers provide to help you succeed in your exam.
- If you have a disability, ensure that your module or course leader is aware as soon as possible so that any reasonable adjustments can be made.
- Be sure about whether you are taking a formative or summative attempt.
- Ensure you know how many attempts you are able to undertake.
- Aim to work out your own learning style.
- Identify which areas from your learning style analysis you can develop further.

4 What to expect from your OSCE

Summary

- You should have an idea of the room and station layout before you start the OSCE.
- You should be aware of and familiar with any equipment or documentation you will be required to use.
- You should understand the set guidelines and protocols for your OSCE.
- You need to behave in a professional manner at all times during your OSCE.
- Your models may be members of the general public, staff, manikins or task trainers.
- All patient models will be working to the same ground rules to ensure parity.
- The examination process is governed by strict quality assurance mechanisms to ensure objectivity.
- You may be videoed during the examination for quality assurance and also for feedback for you to learn from.
- Try not to use jargon that the patient may not understand.
- If you feel you have not been treated fairly, you may be able to access a video recording of the event and review how you performed.

- Ensure you find out prior to the OSCE what type of simulated patient you will have to perform your OSCE on. Will it be a live model or a manikin?
- If you are required to perform any aspect of your OSCE using a manikin or task trainer, ensure you ascertain which one you will be using and that you are familiar with it and practise performing the skills using it.
- Although you are being watched closely, being well prepared helps you to overcome any nerves this causes.
- Find out if your OSCE will be video-recorded and, if so, will an examiner be there as well?
- If you are required to sit a multiple choice or short answer paper as part of your OSCE, ensure you access and complete some practice papers prior to your OSCE.
- The examiner is not trying to be intimidating, however, they have to act professionally during the OSCE and ensure that they treat each student the same.

5 Preparing for your OSCE

Summary

- Remember the five Ps: prior preparation prevents poor performance.
- Plan your revision strategy and use the tools for time management.
- Ensure your strategy gives you ample time to revise early and often.
- Maximize your potential by ensuring you eat, drink and relax to minimize any threat to your brain.
- Try revising with fellow students.
- Recognize excessive stress, and reduce any unnecessary stress.
- Read all your instructions well in advance.
- Plan your route to the OSCE so you arrive in plenty of time.
- Make the most of the time allocated to you.
- If your mind goes blank during the exam, step back for a few seconds to gather your thoughts.

Tips and key points

- Prior preparation prevents poor performance.
- Your motivation to learn may be just to pass the OSCE, but try to be both intrinsically and extrinsically motivated!
- Make good use of all the help available to help you prepare well.
- The body needs to return to normal following stress to prevent chronic stress and its side-effects.
- Utilize the following 10 simple steps:
  - get organized;
  - understand the assessment;
  - start studying early;
  - review lecture notes;
  - review relevant texts;
  - get answers to your questions;
  - quiz yourself;
  - find a study buddy;
  - attend any formative or OSCE preparation sessions;
  - relax.

Top tips to help you sleep:

- gather together what you will need to take into the exam room (pens, water, allowed texts, calculator, student card etc.);
- stop revising 90 minutes before preparing for bed;
- relax with friends, music, book, TV, etc.;
- have a warm bath or shower;
- use a relaxation exercise;
- if your head's still buzzing with thoughts in the middle of the night, have a notebook by the side of the bed and write them down.

On the day

- Even though you may be nervous or worried, listen to what the examiner in charge tells you to do. If unsure, ask for clarification.
- Get into role and remember you are a health care professional as well as a student; this may help you with your performance.

- Remember to take your time. Often when nerves set in we rush, and this is when we make mistakes. You have been allocated a certain amount of time as this is how much the examiners feel you will need. Therefore, use this time wisely, take your time, remember the examiner is observing your skills and attitude and will also be assessing your level of knowledge.
- Ensure you carry out a performance and perform every step to the highest quality possible.
- If applicable, ensure you gain consent prior to starting the scenario. Use this opportunity to explain what the procedure will involve.
- Narrate your way through the exam as this will show the examiner you not only know what to do but you know why you are doing it.
- To demonstrate your knowledge base, ensure you relate theory to practice through your narration, and if applicable offer differential diagnosis and normal and abnormal pathology.
- If you have a viva or paper exam as part of your OSCE, ensure you read or listen to the instructions carefully. Before looking at the actual questions, read the instructions: are there any compulsory questions? Marks are often lost by nervous or over-confident students who overlook instructions.
- Read through the paper once and then reread each question. You might think a topic you've revised hasn't come up, when it is there but the wording is unusual.
- If you are being asked questions during the OSCE or as part of a viva and you do not know the answer instantly, you can ask the examiner to repeat the question. This will give you thinking time and also the opportunity to hear the question again. You may pick up key words that you did not register the first time.
- If your mind goes blank during the OSCE, inform the examiner that you just need to step back and take a few seconds to gather your thoughts. You are better off doing this than going on with the exam and making an error.
- If you think that something is wrong, if you feel unwell, or if something is distracting you, inform your examiner.
- Make sure you do not communicate with, or look at, any other candidate. You can be disqualified if you break the exam rules in any way.
- If you finish early, just spend a few seconds going through what you have done – have you missed anything? You can often rectify the situation if you are within the time, however, once you have left the room, you cannot return.

6 Sample OSCEs

Summary

- Fully read any documentation or guidelines given to you before the OSCE.
- Set yourself a date when you can sit down and work through the documentation. You could do this on your own or with your peers.
- Ensure you have an understanding of the complexities of your OSCE.
- Ensure you are fully aware of all the possible components of the OSCE assessment to which you may be exposed.
- Ensure you are aware of the minimum standard of competency you will have to demonstrate to pass your OSCE and aim to achieve *above* this.
- Examine your OSCE checklists and any marking criteria, and make sure that you read them thoroughly, ensuring you understand the key components of your OSCE.
- Identify any areas that seem unclear. These are the areas that you really need to clarify and understand before the OSCE, therefore ensure you ask for clarification from your tutor or examiner.
- The OSCE checklist and marking criteria should be used to help you prepare and succeed in your exam.
- Confirm whether the OSCE is pass/fail or has a grade attached to it.
- The key to success is practice, practice and more practice.

7 After the OSCE

Summary

- Find out when you can expect to receive feedback on your performance in the OSCE.
- Find out in what format(s) you will receive your feedback.
- Engage in your feedback, even if you passed.
- Highlight any comments that you feel would be useful in future OSCEs.
- Reflect on your performance and the feedback given.
- Aim to reflect with your peers to prevent you engaging in self-affirmation.
- Act upon your reflection.
- If you do not understand any of the feedback, ask for clarification.
- If you fail your exam, ensure you seek support and take up any extra support that is offered.
- Engage in evaluation of your OSCE process to help to improve the experience for others.

Tips and key points

- There is sometimes quite a gap between what your tutors are expecting of you and what you think you need to achieve.
- Clarify verbally, in writing, and by example from your tutors, exactly what is being looked for and assessed in your OSCE.
- Reflection takes courage. To make it meaningful you need to open up your practice to critiquing and examination by others as well as yourself.
- Feedback needs to be timely and occur soon after your OSCE to be most valuable.
- Ask for feedback regularly to improve your practice most effectively.
- Having a good dialogue with your tutor will help you to feel more of a partner in your feedback.
- Listen to your fellow students and gain good feedback and encouragement to improve in your OSCE.
- Don't compare your marks with others – concentrate instead on making your own performance better.
- Work on being a person who sees themselves as someone who can always change and improve and does not have a fixed ability level.
- Aim to attend any extra support sessions to gain the maximum amount of practice time for your OSCE.
- Put an action plan into place and highlight comments for future OSCEs.

Good luck from the authors for all of your future OSCEs!

References

Alinier, G. (2003) Nursing students' and lecturers' perspectives of objective structured clinical examination incorporating simulation, *Nurse Education Today*, 23: 419–26.

Baume, D. (2004) A dynamic theory of organizational knowledge creation, *Organization Science*, 5: 14–37.

Benner, P. (1984) *From Novice to Expert: Excellence and Power in Clinical Nursing Practice*. Menlo Park, CA: Addison-Wesley.

Bloom, B.S. (1956) *Taxonomy of Educational Objectives, Handbook I: The Cognitive Domain*. New York: David McKay.

Borton, T. (1970) *Reach, Touch and Teach*. London: McGraw-Hill.

Boud, D. and Brew, A. (1995) Developing a typology for learner self assessment practices, *Research and Development in Higher Education*, 18: 130–5.

Boyle, J.T. and Nicol, D.J. (2003) Using classroom communication systems to support interaction and discussion in large class settings, *Association for Learning Technology Journal*, 11(3): 43–57.

Bradshaw, A. and Merriman, C. (2008) Nursing competence 10 years on: fit for practice or purpose yet? *Journal of Clinical Nursing*, 17(10): 1263–9.

Bramble, K. (1994) Nurse practitioners' education: enhancing performance through the use of the OSCE, *Journal of Nursing Education*, 22(2): 59–65.

Brookes, G. (2004) Assessment of student advanced neonatal nurse practitioners in resuscitation and stabilization of the newborn: the use of the OSCE, *Journal of Neonatal Nursing*, 10(6): 184–7.

Bujack, L., McMillan, M., Dwyer, J. and Hazelton, M. (1991) Assessing comprehensive nursing performance: the OSCE, part 2, report of the evaluation project, *Nurse Education Today*, 11: 248–55.

Bulman, C. and Schutz, S. (2008) *Reflective Practice in Nursing*, 4th edn. Oxford: Blackwell.

Butler, R. (1988) Enhancing and undermining intrinsic motivation: the effects of task-involving and ego-involving evaluation on interest and involvement, *British Journal of Educational Psychology*, 58: 1–14.

Carraccio, C. and Englander, R. (2000) The objective structured clinical examination: a step in the direction of competency-based evaluation, *Archives of Paediatrics Adolescent Medicine*, 154(July): 736–41.

Channock, K. (2000) Comments on essays: do students understand what tutors write? *Teaching in Higher Education*, 5(1): 95–105.

Chatterjee, M. (2004) Are skills labs a true training ground? *Nursing Times*, 100(24): 12–21.

DoH (Department of Health) (1999) *Making a Difference: Strengthening the Nursing, Midwifery and Health Visiting Contribution to Health and Healthcare*. London: DoH.

DoH (Department of Health) (2007) *Essence of Care: Patient-focused Benchmarks for Clinical Governance*. London: NHS Modernization Agency.

Dreyfus, H.L. and Dreyfus, S.E. (1986) *Mind over Machine: The Power of Human Intuition and Expertise in the Era of the Computer*. Oxford: Blackwell.

Dweck, C. (1999) *Self Theories: Their Role in Motivation, Personality and Development*. Philadelphia, PA: Psychology Press.

Freeman, R. and Lewis, R. (1998) *Planning and Implementing Assessment*. London: Kogan Page.

Fry, H., Ketteridge, S. and Marshall, S. (2001) *A Handbook for Teaching and Learning in Higher Education*. London: Kogan Page.

Furlong, E., Fox, P., Lavin, M. and Collins, R. (2005) Oncology nursing students' views of a modified OSCE, *European Journal of Oncology Nursing*, 8(4): 283–4.

Gibbs, G., Farmer, B. and Eastcote, D. (1988) *Learning by Doing: A Guide to Teaching and Learning Methods*. Birmingham: FEU, Birmingham Polytechnic.

Gibbs, G. and Simpson, C. (2004) Conditions under which assessment supports students' learning, *Learning and Teaching in Higher Education*, 1: 3–31.

Gordon Training International (1970s) *Teacher Effectiveness Training Instructor Guide*. West Solana Beach, CA: Gordon Training International.

Govaerts, M., Schuwirth, L., Pin, A., Clement, M. and van der Vleuten, C. (2001) Objective assessment is needed to ensure competence, *British Journal of Midwifery*, 9(3): 156–61.

Hall, W. (2006) Developing clinical placements in times of scarcity, *Nurse Education Today*, 26: 627–33.

Harden, R.M. and Gleeson, F.A. (1979) Assessment of clinical competence using an objective structured clinical examination (OSCE), *Medical Education*, 13: 41–54.

Hilton, P.A. and Pollard, C.L. (2004) Supporting clinical students' development, *Nursing Standard*, 18(35): 31–6.

Hodges, B. (2003) Validity and the OSCE, *Medical Teacher*, 25(3): 250–4.

Hounsell, D. (1997) Contrasting conceptions of essay writing, in F. Marton, D. Hounsell and N. Entwistle (eds) *The Experience of Learning*, 2nd edn. Edinburgh: Scottish Academic Press.

Howell, W.C. and Fleishman, E.A. (eds) (1982) *Human Performance and Productivity, Vol. 2: Information Processing and Decision Making*. Hillsdale, NJ: Lawrence Erlbaum.

Hulett, S. and Gilder, N. (1986) The application and development of the objective structured practical examination in evaluating physiotherapy students' performance at the University of Cape Town, *South African Journal of Physiotherapy*, 42(2): 40–3.

Hyland, P. (2000) Learning from feedback on assessment, in A. Booth and P. Hyland (eds) *The Practice of University History Teaching*. Manchester: Manchester University Press.

Jasper, M. (2003) *Beginning Reflective Practice*. Cheltenham: Nelson Thornes.

Johns, C. (2000) *Becoming a Reflective Practitioner: A Reflective and Holistic Approach to Clinical Nursing, Practice Developments and Clinical Supervision*. Oxford: Blackwell Science.

Khattab, A. and Rawlings, B. (2001) Assessing nurse practitioner students using a modified objective structured clinical examination (OSCE), *Nurse Education Today*, 18: 441–7.

Knight, C. (1998) Evaluating a skills centre: the acquisition of psychomotor skills in nursing, a review of the literature, *Nursing Education Today*, 18: 441–7.

Knight, C. and Mowforth, G. (1998) Skills centre: why we did it, how we did it, *Nurse Education Today*, 18: 389–93.

Laurillard, D. (2002) *Rethinking University Teaching: A Controversial Framework for the Effective Use of Learning Technologies*, 2nd edn. London: Routledge Falmer.

Major, D. (2005) OSCEs – seven years on the bandwagon: the progress of an objective structured clinical evaluation programme, *Nurse Education Today*, 25: 442–54.

Marshall, G. and Harris, P. (2000) A study of the role of an objective structured clinical examination in assessing clinical competence in third-year student radiographers, *Radiography*, 6: 117–22.

Merriman, C. (2007) What are third year pre-registration adult student nurses' experiences and perceptions of Objective Structured Clinical Examinations (OSCEs) as an assessment strategy? Unpublished MSc dissertation, Oxford Brookes University.

Mossey, P., Newton, J. and Stirrups, D. (2001) Scope of the OSCE in the assessment of clinical skills in dentistry, *British Dental Journal*, 190(6): 323–6.

National Review of Nurse Education Australia (2002) *Our Duty of Care*. Canberra: Department of Education, Science and Training.

Nicol, D.J. and Macfarlane-Dick, D. (2006) Formative assessment and self-regulated learning: a model and seven principles of good feedback practice, *Studies in Higher Education*, 31(2): 199–218.

Nicol, M. and Freeth, D. (1998) Assessment of clinical skill: a new approach to an old problem, *Nurse Education Today*, 16: 121–6.

NMC (Nursing and Midwifery Council) (2004) *Standards of Proficiency for Pre-registration Nursing Education*. London: NMC.

NMC (Nursing and Midwifery Council) (2007a) *Introduction of Essential Skills Clusters for Pre-registration Nursing Programmes*, circular 07/07, plus annexe 1 and 2. London: NMC.

NMC (Nursing and Midwifery Council) (2007b) *Essential Skills Clusters, for pre-registration Nursing Programmes*, circular 07/2007, annexe 1 and annexe 213, updated 7 March 2008. London: NMC.

NMC (Nursing and Midwifery Council) (2007c) *Supporting Direct Care through Simulation Practice Learning in Pre-registration Nursing Programme*, NMC circular 36. London: NMC.

NMC (Nursing and Midwifery Council) (2008a) *The Code: Standards of Conduct, Performance and Ethics for Nurses and Midwives*. London: NMC.

NMC (Nursing Midwifery Council) (2008b) *Standards for Medicines Management*. London: NMC, www.nmc-uk.org/aArticle.aspx?ArticleID=3958, accessed 11 February 2010.

Norton, L.S. (1990) Essay writing: what really counts? *Higher Education*, 20(4): 411–42.

O'Neill, A. and McCall, J. (1996) Objectively assessing nursing practices: a curricular development, *Nurse Education Today*, 16: 121–6.

Orsmond, P., Merr, S. and Reiling, K. (2002) The use of formative feedback when using student derived marking criteria in peer and self-assessment, *Assessment & Evaluation in Higher Education*, 27(4): 309–75.

QAA (Quality Assurance Agency) (1999) Code of Practice for the Assurance of Academic Quality and Standards in Higher Education, www.qaa.ac.uk/academicinfrastructure/codeOfPractice/section3/default.asp, accessed 10 May 2010.

Quinn, F. (2000) *Principles and Practice of Nurse Education*, 4th edn. Cheltenham: Nelson Thornes.

Ramsden, P. (2002) *Learning to Teach in Higher Education*. London: Routledge Falmer.

Redfern, S., Norman, I., Calman, L., Watson, R. and Murrell, A. (2002) Assessing competence to practise: a review of the literature, *Research Papers in Education*, 17(1): 51–77.

Regehr, G., MacRae, H., Reznick, R. and Szalay, D. (1998) Comparing the psychometric properties of checklists and global rating scales for assessing performance on an OSCE format examination, *Academic Medicine*, (73): 993–7.

Reznick, R., Regehr, G., Yee, G., Rothman, A., Blackmore, D. and Dauphinee, D. (1998) Process rating forms versus task-specific checklists in an OSCE for medical insurance, *Academic Medicine*, 73: 97–9.

Rolfe, G., Freshwater, D. and Jasper, M. (2001) *Critical Reflection for Nursing and the Helping Professions*. Basingstoke: Palgrave Macmillan.

Ross, M., Carroll, G., Knight, J., Chamberlain, M., Forthergill-Bourbonnais, F. and Linton, J. (1988) Using the OSCE to measure clinical skills performance in nursing, *Journal of Advanced Nursing*, 13: 45–56.

Rust, C., Price, M. and O'Donovan, B. (2003) Improving students' learning by developing their understanding of assessment criteria and processes, *Assessment and Evaluation in Higher Education*, 28(2): 147–64.

Scott, E. (2008) Cortisol and stress: how to stay healthy, *About.com Guide*, updated February 2008.

Shanley, E. (2001) Misplaced confidence in a profession's ability to safeguard the public? *Nurse Education Today*, 21: 136–42.

Singleton, C.H. (chair) (1999) *Dyslexia in Higher Education: Policy, Provision and Practice*. Report of the National Working Party on Dyslexia in Higher Education. Hull: University of Hull on behalf of the Higher Education Funding Councils of England and Scotland.

Studdy, S., Nicol, M. and Fox-Hilary, A. (1994) Teaching and learning clinical skills, Part 1: development of a multidisciplinary skills centre, *Nurse Education Today*, 14: 177–85.

Walters, J. and Adams, J. (2002) A child health nursing objective structured clinical examination (OSCE), *Nurse Education in Practice*, 2: 224–9.

Waugh, A. and Grant, A. (2006) *Ross and Wilson: Anatomy and Physiology in Health and Illness*, 10th edn. Philadelphia, PA: Elsevier.

While, A. (1994) Competence versus performance: which is more important?, *Journal of Advanced Nursing*, 20: 525–31.

Wiggins, G. (1998) *Educative Assessment: Designing Assessments to Inform and Improve Student Performance*. San Francisco: Jossey-Bass.

Wilson, M., Shepherd, I., Kelly, C. and Pitzner, J. (2005) Assessment of low fidelity human patient simulator for the acquisition of nursing skills, *Nurse Education Today*, 25: 56–67.

Index

Locators shown in *italics* refer to diagrams, figures and tables.

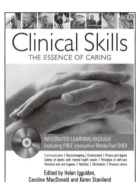

CLINICAL SKILLS
The Essence of Caring

Helen Iggulden, Caroline MacDonald and Karen Staniland

9780335223558 (Paperback)
2009

eBook also available

Clinical Skills: The Essence of Caring is an innovative textbook and integrated Media Tool package which makes teaching and learning nursing interactive! Based on the Essence of Care, this book covers the core clinical skills curriculum and takes a holistic approach to the importance of delivering excellent nursing care

Key features:

- Provides a comprehensive coverage of all the required fundamental skills
- Includes a multitude of activity and case study boxes
- Features a DVD which offers a wealth of fully integrated interactive material, including case studies, skill sets and chapter resources

www.openup.co.uk    OPEN UNIVERSITY PRESS
McGraw - Hill Education